The Trial Of Governor T. Picton: For Inflicting The Torture On Louisa Calderon, A Free Mulatto, And One Of His Britannic Majesty's Subjects, In The Island Of Trinidad, Tried Before Lord Chief Justice Ellenborough And A Special Jury, And Found Guilty

Sir Thomas Picton

THE TRIAL

OF

GOVERNOR T. PICTON,

FOR

INFLICTING THE TORTURE

ON

LOUISA CALDERON,

A Free Mulatto,

AND ONE OF HIS BRITANNIC MAJESTY'S SUBJECTS,

IN THE

ISLAND OF TRINIDAD.

TRIED BEFORE

LORD CHIEF JUSTICE ELLENBOROUGH

AND A SPECIAL JURY,

AND

FOUND GUILTY.

Taken in Short-Hand during the Proceedings on
the 24th of February, 1806.

LONDON:

Printed by Dewick & Clarke, Aldersgate-street,

FOR B. CROSBY AND CO. STATIONERS'-COURT, PATERNOSTER-ROW;
W. JONES AND J. JONES, LIVERPOOL; MOTTLEY, PORTSMOUTH;
LEGG AND MARTIN, GOSPORT; ROACH AND HOXLAND,
DOCK; ROGERS, GRAY, HAYDEN, AND CO. PLYMOUTH;
And all other Booksellers.

THE TRIAL

OF

BRIG. GEN. T. PICTON.

AFTER the counts of the indictment were generally stated by Mr. Harrison,

Mr. Garrow opened the case on the part of the prosecution in the following terms. " The task of stating the particulars in this transaction, so extraordinary in its nature, and so singular in the circumstances with which it was attended, had been committed to much abler hands than those to which it has unfortunately devolved. But it is happy for me that, difficult as the duty may appear to my inferior abilities, the very peculiarity of the transaction, surrounded as it is by all its horrid accompaniments, renders eloquence wholly unnecessary, when the facts are submitted to the consideration of a British jury. Unless, gentlemen, the facts clearly and fully substantiated before you force from you a reluctant verdict of guilty, I have no difficulty in saying that the defendant ought not to be convicted: I call it a reluctant verdict, because there is no individual present,

B

not even he who is appointed to prosecute, who would not, on such an occasion, hear the verdict with extreme reluctance. In the progress of this trial, we shall learn that a governor of one of our colonial dependencies has abused the situation to which he was raised, and has disgraced the country to which he belonged, by inflicting torture upon one of His Majesty's subjects, without the least motive but to gratify a tyrannical disposition, to oppress an unfortunate and defenceless victim of his cruelty.

" Gentlemen, the island of Trinidad surrendered to an illustrious officer, whose name must be ever mentioned with respect and gratitude, in the year 1797. That great man, Sir Ralph Abercrombie, entered into stipulations, by which he conceded to the inhabitants of this Spanish settlement, the continuance of their laws and institutions, and he appointed a new governor until His Majesty's pleasure should be known; or, in other words, until the Sovereign of Great Britain had, in his paternal kindness towards this new dependence of his empire, extended to it all the privileges and advantages of English laws.

" I have the authority of the defendant himself for stating, that previous to his introduction to the government, the juridical regulations of the Spanish monarch were mild and benignant, and adapted to the protection of the subject under his peculiar situation in this remote insular establishment.

" Louisa Calderon, on whose treatment the present prosecution is founded, was of the age of ten or eleven years, when she was induced to live with a person of the name of Pedro Ruiz in the character of his mistress. With our habits it appears very extraordinary that she should be in such a situation at this tender period of life, but in that hot country the puberty of females is much accelerated, and they become mothers frequently when they are only twelve years old. While the young woman lived with Ruiz, she was engaged in an intrigue with Carlos Gonzalez, who robbed his friend of a quantity of dollars, and was in consequence taken into custody. Under these circumstances, some suspicions fell upon her, and she was taken before the magistrate or justice, as we should call this officer of the laws in this country. On her examination before this person, she denied having any knowledge or concern in the transaction; and whether this denial was to protect herself, or her friend, from injurious consequences, it is not at all material to enquire. Thus resisted in his endeavours to discover the truth, the magistrate felt that his powers were at an end—that he had no authority to take any coersive means to extort confession, and he therefore resorted to the defendant, who was invested with the supremacy of the island, to supply the deficiency; and, gentlemen, I have to produce, in the hand-writing of General Picton himself, this bloody sentence:

' Inflict the torture on Louisa Calderon.'

" You will readily believe that there was no unnecessary delay in proceeding to its execution. The girl was told in the gaol, that if she would not make her confession, she would be put to the torture, and that if she suffered the loss of a limb or life during the experiment, the consequences would be on her own head; but that if she would confess, she would avoid the punishment. In order to operate on her imagination, two or three negresses were brought before her in the apartment where torture was usually applied, and these unhappy wretches were to suffer the horrid ceremony under a charge of witchcraft, and as a means of extorting confession. All this host of preparation had not sufficient effect upon her fears, and she resolutely persisted in her innocence, and the punishment was applied which has been improperly called piqueting. I say improperly, because piqueting is a military punishment, but this is properly distinguished by the name of the torture. True it is, that there is some resemblance between the one practice and the other; in both cases the foot is placed upon a sharp wooden point, but in the former mercy has assigned for the sufferer a means of reposing or raising himself by the interior of his arm, by which the agony to the foot is diminished. Not only for the sake of correctness, but for the sake of humanity, I hope this practice will not recieve the appellation of *picqueting*, but that of *pictoning*, that it may be known by the most horrid name by which

2

shew that he possessed no controul, and that he was impelled by irresistible necessity.

"What was the language of our legal institutions, as they were explained by a learned and elegant writer, when adverting to this subject?"

" The trial by rack is utterly unknown to the law of England, though once, when the Dukes of Exeter and Suffolk, and other ministers of Henry VI. had laid a design to introduce the civil law into this kingdom, as the rule of government, for a begining thereof, they erected a rack for torture, which was called in derision, the Duke of Exeters daughter, and still remains in the Tower of London, where it was occasionally used as an engine of state, not of law, more than once in the reign of Queen Elizabeth. But when, upon the assassination of Villiers, Duke of Buckingham, by Felton, it was proposed in the Privy Council, to put the assassin to the rack, in order to discover his accomplices, the Judges, being consulted, declared unanimously. To their own honour, and the honour of the English law, that no such proceeding was allowable by the laws of England." (Black: Comm: b. 4. c. 25.)

" The subject has been reduced into the form of a mathematical problem. The force of the muscles, and the sensibility of the nerves of an innocent person being given, it is required to find the degree of pain, necessary to make him confess himself guilty of a given crime.'

" What are we to say of this defendant, who, so

far from having found torture in practice under the former governors, has attached to himself, all the infamy of having invented this instrument of cruelty? Like the Duke of Exeter's daughter, it never had existence until the defendant cursed the island with its production. I have incontestible evidence to shew this ingenuity of tyranny in a British governor, and the moment I produce the sanguinary order, the man is left absolutely without defence. The date of the transaction is removed at some distance. It was directed that a commission should conduct the affairs of the government, and among the persons appointed to this important situation, was Colonel Fullarton.* In the exercise of his important functions, he attained the knowledge of these facts, and, with this information, he thought it incumbent on him to bring the defendant before you, and, with the defendant, I shall produce the victim of his enormity, whom, from the accident of my being conducted to a consultation into a room by mistake, I have myself seen. She will be presented before you, and you will learn she at this moment

---

* When it was known that commissioners, were appointed, and that Colonel Fullarton was the senior one, the inhabitants became almost delirious with joy, at the bare idea of being soon relieved from oppression. Hence they also became strongly prejudiced in his favour, long before he arrived, conceiving he would bring with him, what was much wanted in the colony, i. e. justice, humanity, protection, and happiness.—See Travels in Trinidad by Pierre F: Mc. Cullum. Sold by Messrs. B. Crosby & Co. Stationers Court, Ludgate Hill.

bears about her the marks of the barbarity of the defendant. In due time you will hear what my excellent and amiable friend near me has to offer in behalf of his client; I state the case at present with full confidence in your verdict; I ask nothing from your passions; nothing but justice do I require, and I have no doubt, at the conclusion of this trial, that you will be found to have faithfully executed your duty.

WITNESSES FOR THE CROWN.

Lousia Calderon appeared on being called by Mr. Adam. She was attended by two interpreters, the one for the Spanish language, the other for the Creole corruptions, or variations from that language.

Q. Were you at the island of Trinidad in the year 1798? A. I was.

Q. Were you acquainted with Pedro Ruiz? A. Yes.

Q. Did you live in his house? A. I did.

Q. At what time did you first go to live with him? A. I do not know the year.

Q. Were you there in 1799 and 1800? A. I cannot positively say I was, for I am not used to distinguish the years in this way.

Q. Were you there at the time the defendant was governor of the island? A. I was there when General Picton was governor.

Q. Do you remember that a robbery was committed in the house of Pedro Ruiz? A. I do.

Q. Who was the person suspected of having committed it? A. Carlos. (Gonzalez.)

Q. Do you remember his being taken up, and sent to prison for the robbery? A. Yes.

Q. Were you and your mother also apprehended on suspicion of being concerned in it? A. Yes the same night.

Q. Who were you carried before? A. Before Mr. Picton.

Q. Did he order you to be committed to prison? A. Yes, I was sent by his orders.

Q. Under what guard were you sent? Did not some soldiers attend you? A. Yes, three soldiers.

Q Were you in close confinement at the prison? A. I was sent to the woman's side.

Q. Before you were sent to prison, did the defendant say any thing to you? A. The governor said, that if I would not confess, the hangman was to put his hand upon me.

Q. Did he say nothing more? A. No more, but he sent me to prison.

Q. Do you know a man of the name of Begorat? A. I do.

Q. Was he an Alcalde*on the island? A. Yes, he was.

* *Alcalde* is a magistrate of which there are several distinctions. 1 *Alcalde de Aldéa,* A Mayor, Bailiff, or Headborough of a country town. 2 *Alcalde Mayor de Justicia,* A Lord Chief Justice. 3 *Alcalde de Corte,* A Judge belonging to the King's household. 4 *Alcalde de Alcades.* The High commissioner over the Justices. 5 *Alcalde de las Alcadas,* A Judge of Appeals from imferior Courts. 6 *Alcalde de los Hidalgos,* A Judge to try the rank of a party, to ascertain if he be exonerated from certain taxes, arrests, &c.

A. Yes.

Q. Were you at any time drawn by the pulley, so as to raise you higher? A. Yes.

Q. Had you seen any other persons placed in the same situations before you were? A. Yes, two others.

Q. What effect had this torture upon your body? A. It occasioned a great deal of pain.

Q. What was the effect upon your wrist? A. It was very much swelled.

Q. And upon your foot? A. It was in the same condition.

Q. Were you required to make confession of the robbery while you were tied up? A. I was. Begorat asked if I would confess who took the money.

Q. Were you sworn upon the Holy Evangelists before you were tied up? A. No.

Q. Was there any oath, in any form administered to you? A. No, but I had the Holy Cross held up before me.

Q. What did you say with respect to the robbery at this time? A. While I was suspended, I declared to Señor Begorat, that Carlos (Gonzalez) had taken the money.

Q. Do you recollect if you were tied up the first time on the 23rd of December, 1801? A. I cannot remember the particular day.

Q. Was it in that month? A. I know it was done eleven days after I had been sent to prison.

Q. Were you sent there about Christmas-time?
A. Yes.

Q. When you were taken down, what did they do with you? A. They took me into a lower room called Ballo's room.

Q. Who was Ballo? A. The goaler.

Q. Why were you taken there? A. That I might own to Ballo, who had robbed Ruiz of the money.

Q. Did you see Carlos there? A. Carlos was there.

Q. How long were you in the goalers room? A. I do not know.

Q. Were you there all night? A. No.

Q. Were did you go after you left the goaler's room? A. into the same room where I had been tortured.

Q. Where you kept there all night? A. Yes.

Q. Where you put in irons? A. Yes, I was in the grillos,* or fetters.

Q. Describe the grillos? A. They consist of a piece of wood, with two iron rings for the legs.

Q. Had you this on all night? A. I was fastened to the bar all the night.

The counsel for the prosecution produced a drawing in ink of this machine, which the witness said was a just representation of it, and it seemed precisely to answer her description,]

Q. Were you put upon the picquet again the next day? A. I was.

* Fetters for the legs.

Q. Upon the same instrument of torture, and in the same manner? A. I was.

Q. At what time of the day? A. It was in the morning.

Q. How long were you kept upon the instrument? A. Twenty-two minutes.

Q. Was there a watch placed near to ascertain the time? A. Yes.

Q. Who were present on the second day? A The Alcalde Begorat and Francisco de Castro were there.

Q. Were there others present? A. there was Rafael an Alguazil.*

Q. With which arm were you tied up on the second day? A. By both arms, one after the other.

Q. Were you drawn up by the rope, and pulley the second day, so as to remove your foot from the spike of wood? A. No, I could just touch it with the end of my toe.

Q. Your shoes were off both days? A. Yes.

Q. Your feet were naked, I suppose? (Question by his Lordship) A. Yes there were.

Q. What effect did this state of suffering produce? A. I fainted away.

Q. On both days? (Question by his Lordship.) A. No, only on the second day.

Q. Were you taken down upon your fainting? A. I do not know.

* Alguazil is the name of an officer for the apprehension of criminals.

Q. Does your ignorance arise from your state of insensibility at the time, or has the circumstance escaped your memory ?   A. I do not recollect any thing about it.

Q. Did they take you down before, or subsequent to your fainting?   A. I cannot at all tell.

Q. Did they give you any thing to conduce to your recovery?   A. Ballo applied vinegar to my nostrils.

Q. To what place were you conveyed afterwards ?   A. I continued in the apartment where the picquet was.

Q. Were you again put in irons ?   A. Yes in the grillos.

Q. How long after the torture?   A. The same evening.

Q. How long did they keep you in fetters ? A. All the time I was in prison.

Q. How many months was that ?   A. Eight.

Q. Were you ever taken from prison to go to the house of Pedro Ruiz?   A. I was.

Q. How long after the last time of the application of the torture?   A. I remember Begorat took me to the house of Ruiz, but I cannot say at what time.

Q. Was it a month afterwards?   A. I do not know.

Q. Were you able to walk there without assistance?   A. I was very bad; I went all the way quite lame.

Q. To what was the lameness to be attributed ? A. To the irons with which I was fastened.

Q. What age were you when you were confined?
A. Thirteen, and going for fourteen years old.

Q. How came you to be released at the end of eight months? A. I do not know the occasion of my release.

Q. Had Colonel Fullarton arrived in Trinidad before you were liberated? A. I believe he arrived after I was set free.

Q. How soon after? A. I do not know.

Q. Are there any marks of the injury you received from the torture or from the irons now apparent on your body? A. On my hands, but none on my feet.

Q. On one hand, or on both? A. On both my wrists.

[The witness here exhibited a seam or callus, formed on both wrists, which she said was the consequence of the treatment she had received.]

The Witness cross-examined by Mr. Dallas.

Q. How long was it between the time of your release, and your setting out for England? A. I do not recollect.

Q. Was it many months? A. I do not know.

Q. Did you come with Col. Fullarton? A. Yes.

Q. By whom have you been supported in this country? A. By Mr. White. (Of the treasury.)

Q. Who is he? A gentleman living in London.

D

Rafael Shando was next sworn with his Interpreter, and examined by Mr. Garrow.

Q. Were you an Alguazil in the island of Trinidad in the year 1801? A. Yes.

Mr. Dallas, (interposing). " This man has taken the oath, but is he a believer, and acquainted with the solemnity?"

Mr. Garrow continued the examination.

Q. Are you a christian? A. I am.

Q. Do you consider yourself bound to tell the truth, and that you call God to witness that you do so? A. Yes, I do.

Q. Were you sworn in this manner before the Privy Council?A. Yes I was.

Q. Do you remember returning from the country to Puerto de España on the 22nd of December? A. I do.

Q. Do you know Louisa Calderon, a young woman who has been examined? A. Yes.

Q. When you arrived at the goal in Puerto de España did you see her? A. Yes.

Q. Under what circumstances? A. The goaler, Señor Begorat, Francisco de Castro, and Joseph Flores, an Alguazil, were with her.

Q. What were they doing to Louisa Calderon? A. They were giving her a glass of wine and water.

Q. On what account did they give it to her? A. They had just been bringing her down from the torture.

Q. Was she in a state of acute suffering at that time? A. Yes in great pain.

Q. In what attitude was she? A. She was supporting herself on a table.

Q. What time in the evening of the 23rd was it? A. About seven o'clock.

Q. What was done afterwards? A. Begorat interrogated Louisa, and then said to her, you will tell Carlos the same you have told me before? To which she replied yes, Sir.

Q. What was done then? A. Begorat then desired me to fetch Carlos up.

Q. You then brought Carlos into Louisa's presence? A. Yes.

Q. What passed in consequence? A. Nothing then passed.

Q. What was done with Louisa that night? A. She was put in the grillos directly.

[The same drawing of the grillos was now handed to the witness which had been before seen by Louisa Calderon.]

Q. Is that a true description of the irons? A. Yes, exactly.

Q. In what apartment was she confined in these fetters? A. In the same room in which she received the torture.

Q. What was the form of the room? A. It was like a garret, the middle high, and the sides very low.

Q. Was there room for her to sit upright? A. She could not sit upright: where the irons were placed, she was obliged to lye down.

Q. Was she always in this situation? A. Yes, she was so all night and all day, all the time she was in custody.

Q. Was she again put to the torture on the 23rd? A. Yes, Begorat ordered me to go to tell the execntioner to get ready.

Q. When was this? A. The day after the first torture.

Q. Do you know if that was upon the eve of Christmas-day? A. It was the day after the first torture.

Q. What was the time? A. Between eleven and twelve in the morning.

Q. The first torture was finished at seven o'clock the evening before, was it not? A. Yes.

Q. Upon the second day, what was done to Louisa? A. She was again exposed to the torture.

Q. According to what method? A. She was suspended by one wrist, the toe of the opposite foot being at the same time supported by a spike, the other opposite foot and hand were tied together.

Q. Was the foot applied to the spike, in the middle or only the extremity? A. A very small part of the great toe touched the spike.

[The drawing before referred to was now exhibited to the witness, who said it was a just representation of her attitude during the torture.]

Q. How long did she remain in that situation?
A. By my own watch, twenty two minutes.

Q. Did she appear to you to suffer extreme anguish under the torture? A. She fainted twice in my arms.

Q. Was her agony very great? A. She fainted, that is all I can say.

Q. Did she make any application to be relieved, by altering the mode of the torture? A. She fainted while she was tied up, and Begorat sent for vinegar for her, to Ballo the Goaler.

Q. In twenty two minutes she was taken down?
A. Yes.

Q. Could she have borne the suffering any longer?
A. I have said she fainted twice under the pressure of it, and I can add nothing more.

Q. Was there a defensor (advocate) appointed for her, to take care of her interests? A. None.

Q. Who were present during the torture? A. Begorat, Francisco de Castro, Ballo, and myself.

Q. Was there no surgeon present to assist her under the torture? A. No, there were no others present, excepting a negro belonging to Ballo, to pull the rope.

Q. What became of her after she was taken down? A. She was put into fetters directly.

Q. And she continued in this state during eight months? A. Yes.

Q. Was she permitted on any occasions to leave her confinement? A. She once went to the house of Pedro Ruiz, with the goaler and another officer, and with this exception only, she was closely confined for eight months.

Q. Were her friends permitted to come and visit her? A. I have seen the sister bring victuals for her, but never saw the sister admitted into the prison.

Q. How long did you live at Puerto de España? A. About eight years.

Q. Did you live there before the island surrendered to Sir. Ralph Abercrombie? A. Yes.

Q. How long had you been in the office of Alguazil? A. Four or five years.

Q. Did you know of the torture being inflicted until the defendant arrived in the island? A. Never.

Q. Was there, until the defendant arrived, any instrument of torture? A. The first place of torture I saw, was in the barracks among the soldiers.

Q. Was even that erected until the defendant became governor? A. No, never before.

Q. The defendant for the first time ordered this to be constructed in the barrack yard, after he became governor? A. I never saw any before.

Q. How long was it after the instrument had been introduced into the barrack yard, before it was erected in the gaol? A. I cannot tell how long before, but when Louisa was tormented with it, it had been placed in the prison about six months.

Q. Have you known any other instance in which the defendant inflicted the torture? A. I recollect General Picton once said to the goaler, " Go and fetch the black man of the picquet guard, and put him to the torture." This was the first instance of the use of the torture in Trinidad, that I was acquainted with."

Q. Are you sure that there was no instrument of torture in the goal before the time you have spoken to? A. I was in office of justice, and never saw it, I think, until five or six months before Louisa was tormented.

Q. You have said she remained about eight months in confinement: was she ever brought to a trial? A. She was brought to what you call here (and after some hesitation, he added) a parliament.

Q. Both Louisa and Carlos were discharged after a period of about eight months. A. Yes they were.

The Witness cross-examined by Mr. Lawes.

Q. On what occasion was Carlos discharged? A. At the time the judge ordered him to pay the money.

Q. What became of him afterwards? A. He went to Margarita.

Q. By whom was he sent? A. He was sent out of the island, but I do not know by what order.

Juan Montes was then sworn, unassisted by an Interpreter, and was examined by Mr. Harrison.

Q. Are you acquainted with the handwriting of the defendant? A. I am.

[A paper was now shewn to the witness, containing what was stated to be the original order for the application of the torture to Louisa Caldero]

Q. Is the name, subscribed to that paper, the handwriting of the defendant? A. It is.

Q. Is the signature only his handwriting, or the whole of the characters? A. All of them.

Q. Be pleased to read the contents.

" *Apliquese la question a Louisa Calderon.*

(Signed) Thomas Picton."

Mr. Dallas. " I think, my Lord, we are entitled to have the paper read to which this order is an answer."

Mr. Garrow. " I conceive it to be an order unconnected with any application, and having no reference to such application, there is no occasion to introduce it."

Lord Ellenborough. " It is written evidently in consequence of some application, and, if read, we shall have the advantage of having the whole before us."

Mr. Dallas. " That is all, my lord, I can either solicit or desire."

Mr. Garrow. " The matter is certainly not of any importance, but, when I produce in evidence an insulated paper, I am entitled to the privilege of reading it, and nothing more. The paper referred to is merely this: Begorat says, he has no authority to inflict the torture without the consent of the governor. Is not this strictly, my lord, a part of their evidence, and not of mine?"

Mr. DALLAS. "It is of no importance to you to struggle for the reply, for I shall give evidence in behalf of the defendant."

Mr. GARROW. "If it be read, the gentlemen of the jury will recollect that the representation of Begorat proves no fact, excepting that he represents it."

Mr. LOWTON, the clerk of the court, now read the paper referred to, with the consent of his Lordship. It was dated at the Puerto de España, on the 22nd of Dec. 1801, and it stated, in the Spanish language, that his honour, the judge of first appointment, presided at the prison, where Louisa Calderon, a free Mulatto, was confined for the purpose of taking her depositions: that the notary administered the oath in due form in the name of God our Lord, and on the Holy Cross; that she promised to swear the truth, but that she denied any knowledge of the persons who were the perpetrators of the robbery; after which his honour ordered the interrogatories to be suspended. In consequence of the strong suspicions entertained that Louisa Calderon concealed the truth, which his honour was persuaded she would discover by a slight torment, his honour not having power to proceed to this measure, had, therefore, acquainted his excellency the governor of the circumstance, and had inclosed the documents, containing a summary of the proceedings. This

E

paper was signed " Begorat," and countersigned " De Castro."

Then it continues ; " I proceeded to his excellency the governor, and made known to him the act, on which his excellency decreed as follows, which I attest:

' *Apply the torture to Louisa Calderon,*

(Signed)   THOMAS PICTON.'

This additional document was signed only by De Castro, and was dated the 23rd of December.

The order of the judge was thus : " At the port of Spain,, in the Windward Island of Trinidad, his honour, the ordinary judge, has directed slight torment should be inflicted, and has decreed that the same shall be carried into execution without further delay. At the same time, as his honour observes, Louisa Calderon is not of the age of twenty-five years, he reserves the intervention of a guardian or advocate."

MR. GARROW. " Then, my Lord, follows the service of the order, and the act of torment."

LORD ELLENBOROUGH. " Does it appear that the subsequent part was known to the defendant ?"

MR. GARROW. " I do not want it."

MR. HARRISON now resumed his examination of *Juan Montes.*

Q. How long have you known Trinidad? A. Since the year 1793.

Q. In what capacity were you there? A. I was assistant to the engineers.

Q. Were you in any legal situation? A. Before the conquest, I was in the military.

Q. Did you, in the course of your experience, ever know that torture had been applied before the conquest? A. Never.

Q. When was it first introduced? A. After the cession, by order of General Picton.

Q. How long after the conquest? A. The first instance of torture was in 1799.

Q. When was it first resorted to in the gaol?

LORD ELLENBOROUGH (interposing). " Was it first used in the gaol?"

Q. Where was the other instrument of torture? A. In the picquet yard.

Q. You mean where the soldiers live? A. I do.

Q, How long was it between the time it was brought into the picquet yard, and the time it was introduced into the gaol? A. It was brought into the gaol about two years afterwards, in 1801.

MR. GARROW. " I have more witnesses of the first respectability, if the material facts in evidence should be at all disputed."

MR, DALLAS. " I am not at all aware that they will be necessary for the purpose to which you refer."

MR. GARROW. " I do not suppose it will be required that I should prove that General Picton was the governor of the island. This order was given in that character."

Mr. DALLAS. " I shall readily wave the production of this proof."

Mr. GARROW. " This, then, is my case on the part of the crown."

Mr. DALLAS. " It now becomes my duty to address your Lordship and the gentleman of the Jury on behalf of the defendant in answer to this case, which has not been a long one, considering the nature of the charge on the part of the prosecution. I can with perfect truth assure you, that the situation in which I now stand, is not with me a matter of choice: I, have for some time ceased to be in the habit of attending this court, and it will hardly be supposed I feel so much confidence in my own powers, and so little sensibility to the condition of my client, as to have undertaken the arduous task of his defence, if the determination had depended on myself. But it has unfortunately happened, that I have failed in my endeavours to convince General Picton of a truth, with the existence of which every other man would have been satisfied, that my feeble abilities are ill adapted to his defence, and that the consequence of my withdrawing would be, that the duty would devolve upon another much more capable of discharging it, excepting in one respect, in which I shall concede preference to no man. I mean, from the anxiety I feel to render substantial service to this gentleman in his present situation. You are now informed of the reason why I have been selected to appear before you. Yet I hope in explaining my

embarrassment, I shall not be in danger of being misun-
derstood, and that it will not be supposed I mean to
insinuate, that from the nature of the evidence, and
the circumstances of the facts, there are peculiar
difficulties in this cause which would have deterred me
from making the defence, or that from personal feelings
of my own, I should be discouraged by any degree
of unpopularity which may appertain to it. There are
matters, which in common with my friends at the
bar, I could contemplate boldly, and meet manfully;
all I wished was, to have been spared a conflict to
which, from other causes, I feel myself unequal.

" Gentlemen, the case before you is of a novel,
and of an extraordinary nature: nor do I mean to
deny, that in whatever light it is considered, whether with regard to the public, or to the individual,
it is of the greatest magnitude, and importance.
On the one hand, nothing can more concern the
public, that extensive powers should not be
perverted to the purposes of malice and oppression,
and on the other, that the individual should not
suffer, if he have lawfully exercised the authority
with which he was invested. If the defendant
have done nothing more than what he deemed a
faithful discharge of this duty, he should not be
consigned over to ruin, and what is worse, to a mind
like his, to dishonour, by the verdict you shall give:
a verdict, which nothing ought to induce you to find,
I may add from the concession of my learned friend,
unless a statement of facts, supported by incontro-

vertible evidence should reluctantly force it from you."

"It is impossible for me, rising to address you, not to feel myself surrounded and pressed upon by difficulties, which for the sake of impartial justice I would fain remove. I cannot but have felt, that a case of this kind, stated and proved as it has been, with prints and drawings, and acting, which I have now seen for the first time introduced in support of a criminal charge, must even with minds determined on impartiality have occasioned sensations unfavourable to the gentleman for whom I appear."

LORD ELLENBOROUGH. "I would not permit the drawings to be shewn to the Jury, until I had your express permission."

MR. DALLAS. "My Lord, I acknowledge it, and perhaps, therefore, I am not correct in now adverting to any advantage that might have been taken of such a concession.

"Gentlemen of the Jury, I was proceeding to say, that living, as we do, in a country were we have the perfection of human institutions, where the characteristics of our laws are mildness and humanity, I must be aware how difficult it is for us to direct ourselves to a different contemplation of things, and to proceed in our examination of the conduct of the defendant; by the sublime notions of English jurisprudence; but according to principles and practice in a remote part of the world, where the state of society is wholly different

from that which subsists in this country. Hard as
the task may be, I am confident you will endeavour
to divest yourselves of these natural prejudices, that
you may pronounce a calm, discreet, sober, and dis-
passionate verdict. Before I proceed to any statement of what I conceive to be the charge in this
particular case, and which with great deference to my
learned friend, I must say, will require a little more
correct attention, than he has bestowed upon it, I
will begin with a short statement, of what are the
circumstances as they are disclosed by the evidence,
on the part of the prosecution.

" It appears, gentlemen, that some time before the
year 1801, the defendant had been appointed governor of the island of Trinidad, and as such, was not
only clothed with the chief military, but also with
the supreme civil authority. At the close of that
year, viz. in December, it now turns out, that a
robbery had been committed in the dwelling house
of a person named Pedro Ruiz. At the time of the
robbery, Lousia Calderon was a domestic in his
house, living in a state of prostitution with him.
The robbery was to a very considerable extent, and
it was committed by Carlos Gonzalez, with whom
the young person I have named was indulging herself in carnal intercourse, at the time she was mistress to Ruiz. It was therefore such a case as would
have been here a capital offence, by which the
parties would have lost their lives. If in any

charge of this kind, it turns out in England, that the robbery is committed by the servants belonging to the family, the judge who tries the cause, is placed in a most painful situation, because he can rarely exercise his humanity, by interposing in favour of the criminals, and the offence is expiated by an ignominous death.

These are some of the facts, which will more distinctly appear before you in the sequel.

" Under these peculiar circumstances, information was laid before the defendant at the government house, when this young person was brought before him, and when the conversation took place to which she has sworn. In the first instance, all the defendant did, when a capital crime had been committed, was to dismiss the consideration of the subject, and to refer it to the competent and ordinary tribunal of the island. Upon this, the parties were committed under his order, not only this young person, but also her mother, Carlos Gonzalez, and the brother of Pedro Ruiz. They were sent to the prison for the purpose of undergoing examination, before Señor Begorat, whom my learned friend calls a justice of the peace, but whose powers and authority were of a very different nature. But this we will pass over for the present. Thus far upon the information of a capital offence, we learn only with respect to Lousia Calderon, that she was committed to the common prison by General Picton.

" So the case arranges itself on the evidence, as it appears on the part of the prosecution; and you will give me leave to pause here, to point out a distinction which strikes my mind very forcibly. The present charge is not for a conspiracy between the defendant and Begorat, for the purpose of subjecting Louisa Calderon to imprisonment and torture, but instead of attacking the origin of the affair, it breaks in, if I may so express myself, upon the full tide and current of it, and charges upon the defendant, what took place upon the progress of an enquiry into a criminal charge, the first step not being taken by himself. I need hardly remind you, as far as the case is supported by proof, in the present stage of it, that it appears, that before the torture was applied, all the means which the nature of the case admitted of, were resorted to, in order to avoid this consequence. Witness after witness was called, day after day was consumed, and it was only after repeated prevarication, on the part of Lousia, and after the suspicions of the judge were confirmed, that the application was made by Begorat, of which you have heard.

" Gentlemen, you have listened to the representation which Begorat made, to the utility he had in view, from the effects of slight torture, to the order from the defendant, and to the execution of such order under that authority. The whole of the testimony shews that the torture did not originate with the defendant; that all which appears to have been

done was under the representations of the ordinary
criminal judge, before whom the enquiry was conducted, and who was sworn to proceed in the affair
according to the laws of Spain, as established in
this colony. Thus recommended, the plaintiff in-
terposes, and, instead of adopting any thing new,
which might be supposed to be applicable to the
peculiar circumstances of the case, he merely suffers
the law to take its course.

"It is very material that you should attend to
this natural, and almost necessary progress of the
affair, because the case, on the part of the prosecution, grounds itself entirely on malice. In such a
predicament we are led to enquire; where was the
commencement of the malice? The defendant
never issued an order to make the smallest advance
until such time as the question came before him in
the regular and ordinary course, suggested by the
criminal charge. Whether it was right to have
given the order for the application of torture, is a
different consideration. But when we reflect on a
charge of malice, as involved in the affair, it de-
serves our particular notice, that all the defendant
did, in the first instance, was to examine, and then to
confirm a suggestion which was made to him as governor, from the ordinary criminal judge in the court
below. When we advert to these concerns, we should
take care to connect nothing with the conduct of
the defendant, which does not strictly and exclusively
appertain to it; and with this view, I have passed

1

over, without observation, much of what you have heard from the witnesses. How the torture was applied, how often it was repeated, in what particular place, or under what singular circumstances it was inflicted, are matters for which the defendant is in no degree responsible; unless it should have been proved, that the defendant was privy to the mode in which his order was carried into execution. Nothing is more clear, in point of legal principle, than that if, by the law of Spain, the defendant was warranted in issuing the order for the treatment of this young person; should any excesses have been committed in the compliance with it, he is in no degree answerable for those excesses. If then that which was directed to be slight, was, in fact, cruel, and violent, or if the confinement was improperly protracted, these are things for which the persons immediately concerned are liable, but not the defendant. You will distinctly recollect that the case, on the part of the prosecution, has been closed without a single attom of proof, that, for one moment, during the eight months, from the original time of the committment of Louisa Calderon, until her ultimate discharge, the defendant at all interfered in any way, either in the early, or subsequent stage of the proceeding.

" Having given this general summary, I will now intreat your attention to the immediate charges. The indictment contains many different counts, each of which it will be necessary separately to consider, because they stand upon very different grounds. But without going, at present, into the more minute detail, I may state the more comprehensive view of this indictment, which reposes on two broad principles. The first is, that the act done was unlawful, or, in other words, that by the law, which the defendant was sworn to administer, he had no right to order the torture to be applied; and this illegality is supposed in all the counts of the indictment. The first ground, then, upon which the charge stands, is the unlawfulness of the act stated to be done, that is, for torture to be employed in this particular instance. But there is another ground, and which is the main foundation of the charge; that is, that it was not only illegally, but maliciously done, and without any reasonable or probable cause. Now it is evident, that not only by the maxims recognized in laws, but by the plainest principles of reason and common sense, by the most obvious notions of natural right and justice, no cases can be more remote, than that where error is stated, and where malice is charged. It may happen to the most upright judge, even to his lordship, under whose direction I have the honour to address you, that he may mistake the limits of his jurisdiction, and do an act which is unlawful; but it can never happen to such a character, not only to do this unlawfully; but to do it without any probable cause. In the point of view we are to consider this offence, no man can act maliciously, unless he also act unlawfully, and therefore, in the correct consideration of the case, the two must be unavoidably blended, and you must be convinced that they were, before you can in conscience find the defendant guilty, which I confidently trust he will not by your verdict. If it should turn out, in point of fact, by the law of Spain, that this proceeding was lawful in the Governor of Trinidad, there is an end of the whole charge; the illegality of the act, I have said, runs through every count of the indictment, and he must be acquitted on them all.

" What is unlawful in this country, may be correctly lawful according to the jurisprudence of that island; and you cannot convict the general if it should be discovered, that he acted perfectly consistent with that law, which you have heard he was sworn to administer. But supposing even, that he had infringed this law, in the erroneous exercise of its authority, this would be a case perfectly distinct from malice, or from the tyrannical desire to oppress, charged upon him in this particular instance.

" The prominent object to be contemplated upon the present occasion, is the place where the offence was committed. It was in the island of Trinidad, in which it appears the defendant was appointed to the supreme military and civil command; and here it is most important that you should attend to the accompaniments of the scene where the affair was transacted.

" For the purpose of an indictment in England, it is only necessary generally to state, that the act done is unlawful, and then it proceeds to the facts, by which the judge is enabled to examine, if the offence charged be a crime known to the law of England. The moment the facts are proved, the question on the crime is referred to the judge, and he is to state if the facts do, or do not, amount to an offence against the laws. This depends upon his knowledge of the law of England; but in the case where the offence is committed in a remote country, the investigation of the charge depends upon facts, perfectly distinct, and often directly opposite in their application. With respect to the law of Spain, I may say, with great deference, to the noble lord who presides in this court, that of this he is supposed to have no knowledge whatever. You are not then upon the facts, as referable to the law of England, to imagine that the defendant is criminal by the law of Spain. Without adverting to the jurisprudence, established by foreign nations for the government of their colonial dependencies, I may assert, with respect to this kingdom, without going farther, that no two systems of jurisprudence can be more different, than the law which prevails in our islands, and the law recognized here. Ten thousand examples might be adduced from the various systems of political institution, in order to support this reasoning, but I will content myself with stating a single case. I will suppose that of a person residing in the island of St. Vincent's; and after having lawfully filled certain magisterial duties there, he should, on his arrival in this country, be taken into custody, on a charge of maiming and disfiguring a particular individual of that settlement; and you will recollect, gentlemen, that such an offence would be felony according to the law of England. I would then suppose a witness, presenting himself before you, not with the perfect use of his limbs, or even with the possession of them unimpaired like this young woman, but with his nose slit, and with his right hand amputated. You would perhaps learn, that the only offence committed by this maimed and unfortunate object was, that he had obstructed a constable, who ordered him to be flogged, and in consequence of this resistance, so natural, if not justifiable, and for no other reason, you would be told, that his face was thus disfigured, so as to lose the character of humanity, and his body was thus deprived of its most valuable member. I will go farther, and suppose that the person was actually put to death, and the indictment charged the foul crime of murder. Under such circumstances, every man deriving his notions from the law of England would unavoidably exclaim, that the man who has done this, shall surely die. But the defence would be fully adequate to the occasion, and the jury would be told, that by the law of St. Vincent's the prisoner was acquitted."

[The learned counsel here read the law of that settlement: it stated, that if a white person were to be hurt by a slave, such offending slave should have his nose slit, or lose any member, to be cut off at the discretion of two justices.]

" By the law recognized in England, for the government of that island, with the same impunity, a magistrate may order a man to be led to immediate death. Consider now, gentlemen, this girl, who has undergone, comparatively speaking such a mild punishment, and a punishment which is inflicted even in England. In point of enormity, there can be no similarity, standing as she does, in perfect health, and in the full capacity for the employment of her corporeal and mental powers.

" Gentlemen, although it might greatly shock your feelings, if you were sitting here in judgment, on the person I have supposed, having acted as I have represented in the island of St. Vincent's, yet it would be your bounden duty to acquit him: for your decision is to be formed, not on the benignity of English laws, but according to the law of the country where the act is performed. Then the transaction took place we have seen in the island of Trinidad ; where I have no doubt you will permit me to assume for the present that a different law exists from that which is established in this country.

" I shall now enquire a little in what situation the defendant was acting, and the means he enjoyed of obtaining a knowledge of the powers with which he was invested. He was acting at the time in either a civil, or a military capacity. In this island there are various gradations of power, and were I to enquire, if it were within the authority of every constable to order the torture, it would supply very little light on the question you have to try. It is requisite here, that I should advert to the form of the allegation."

LORD ELLENBOROUGH. "The words used were intended to bring the matter under the proper juris-diction."

MR. GARROW. "They are the very words of the act."

MR. DALLAS. "His lordship has observed, that the words used are merely for the purpose of jurisdiction, and to give you this jurisdiction, therefore, the allegation is introduced. But to determine the question on the conduct of the defendant, we must carefully examine the nature of his office, and the precise degree of power which belongs to it.

"Let us for a moment attend to the particular situation of Trinidad, which we have seen, until lately, was a colony of Spain. At different periods, opposite schemes have been alternately adopted and abandoned, with respect to this island, by the mother country. Sometimes the object was to promote an extensive and productive cultivation ; sometimes the wealth of the colony had been disregarded ; but a short time before the capture of Trinidad, they had resorted to a project, which they had not reduced to practice in any other of their settlements. The great principle of Spain with regard to her dependencies, is to promote a system of commerce rigidly exclusive; but latterly, with respect to this place, they pursued a different line of conduct, which they supposed to be more to their interest, as the island of Trinidad was near to numerous small settlements, and in the immediate neighbourhood of the Spanish main, or the extensive districts of the Caraccas.

From this circumstance of locality, the Spaniards converted it into a sort of receptacle for persons who were involved in debt, who were accused of crimes, who were discontented with their native home, and in short, with refugees of every character and description. From this new system of colonial policy, as applied to the island, the population became of a very extraordinary kind; in truth, it is impossible to suppose a collection of inhabitants more dangerous and turbulent than that which occupied the territory of this new acquisition obtained by British valour.

" Who was the defendant at the time the island surrendered ? In a long course of time he had run through all the gradations of military service, with honour to himself, and advantage to his country. In his progress to the rank and reputation he acquired, he was principally patronized by Sir Ralph Abercrombie, whose high character has occasioned the encomium of my learned friend; and has justified the applause of a grateful people. Into the family of Sir Ralph the defendant was received, and by him Mr. Picton was esteemed both as a friend and a soldier. He was the Aid de Camp of this able officer at different times, and upon the capture of Trinidad the defendant was the person to whom Sir Ralph Abercrombie thought fit to entrust the government of the island. Under these circumstances, in the year 1797, the defendant was cloathed with this high authority. He was no civilian, no lawyer; his life had been principally passed in camps; and it became necessary to lay down some rules for him in the administration of civil and criminal justice.

" Before 1797, the mode in which justice was dispensed on the island was as follows. There were officers called Alcaldes and persons holding this situation were the ordinary judges of the penal law. It was their duty to take examinations, to enquire into facts, and after much investigation, to proceed to the ultimate acquittal, or condemnation. But with respect to the person of the criminal, they had no final jurisdiction. They were bound to lay their depositions before the Governor of the island, whose duty it was to submit such representations to the royal Audience of Caraccas on the Spanish main, and from this court, an appeal was allowed to a supreme court in the capital of the parent state, called, the Royal Council of Madrid.

" It has been intimated in the course of the address of my learned friend to you, that the punishment of torture had not been inflicted in the island, but the reason is now assigned, for I have said, with respect to the person of the criminal, the appointed judges had no jurisdiction : the report was laid before the governor, by him it was sent to the Audience of Caraccas, and from thence it was transmitted to the seat of empire. Thus the matter stood, and such was the limit of authority under the Spanish Governor : but when Trinidad became an English dependency under an English governor, it was no longer possible to appeal to the Audience

1

of Caraccas, or to any other superior court in the West Indies, and it became indispensably necessary that the defendant should be the supreme judge in all criminal cases. Sir Ralph Abercrombie was aware of this necessity, and in his instructions for the government of the island, it was directed, that the appeal in all cases should lay to the defendant, and in the event of such appeal, he was to act finally according to his own discretion. It is true, that in civil cases, when the property in dispute exceeded the value of five hundred pounds, there was an appeal allowed to His Majesty in council, but in all criminal cases, he was in the precise situation of the Privy Council as to civil cases.

" Such, then, was the constitution of the island under the Spanish government, and such the alterations made by the instructions of Sir Ralph Abercrombie. These instructions were confirmed by his Sovereign, and under this high order, the defendant was invested with all the judicial powers, to the awful extent of making him the judge of appeal, who was finally to decide in every criminal case.

" Gentlemen, having now stated to you the nature of the transaction, with the law of the island before the introduction of the English, and the changes which took place under the instruction of Sir Ralph Abercrombie, confirmed by the King, I shall now expose to you the ground upon which I conceive the defence to rest. For the sake of order, I will lay before you three distinct propositions.

" The first ground upon which I contend that the defendant is entitled to your acquittal, upon every part of the charge, is this, that by the law of Spain, which he was bound to administer, torture was admissable in this particular instance.

" Strong as I conceive this ground to be, God forbid that the defence of this gentleman should rest upon one ground only. The charge is, that the act was not only unlawfully, but maliciously done, and therefore my second argument is:

" That if it were unlawfully, it was not maliciously done, and without reasonable or probable cause."

LORD ELLENBOROUGH. " Every thing against law is presumed to be malicious."

MR. DALLAS. " Certainly, my Lord, but the question of malice as expressed by acts done without reasonable or probable cause, may be explained by facts, illustrative of that reasonable or probable cause, and according to the facts themselves, the defendant may, or may not be entitled to acquittal. Gentlemen of the Jury, it is impossible for me to anticipate what your opinion will be, before you pronounce your final decision, and therefore I am obliged to provide for the case, on the supposition that you should think that torture by the law of Spain ought not to have been applied. Then I shall contend on the third ground :

" That the defendant in his ignorance of the law of Spain applied the torture, and the charge being thus resolved into mistake or error, the indictment will not lie, or in other words, an erroneous execution of authority is a complete answer to a criminal charge.''

" Upon each of these grounds separately, and upon all of them collectively, I shall submit, under his Lordship's direction, that you ought not to find the defendant guilty.

" First, as to the torture in the light in which it is considered by the law of Spain.

" Accustomed to the feelings of Englishmen, at the sound of the word torture, all our sensibilities take the alarm, because the practice of torture involves in it, those means, at the very statement of which, humanity shudders. God forbid, that I should be called upon to detail to you the horrid catalogue of those means, which the most civilized countries of the world have permitted to be the ordinary practice within their borders : it will be sufficient for me to say, that the punishment inflicted in such cases, were various in their degree, from the slightest to the greatest excess of suffering, which man can endure. And now it becomes expedient to enquire what was the nature, the degree, and the kind of punishment which was applied in this particular instance ; and it is the more necessary, that I should direct your attention to this subject, on account of the florid representation, made by the eloquence of my learned friend, always ardent, always glowing, always possessing that formidable strength, which this master of oratory can so dexterously employ. But he was not content even with the application of his extraordinary powers, he improved the effect by a sort of scenic display."

LORD ELLENBOROUGH. "That you must attribute to me, or perhaps to yourself, for I distinctly asked you whether you would permit the exhibition, and on your concurring, I desired the jury simply to attend to the position of the sufferer, with the view to explain the testimony of the witness."

MR. DALLAS. "I am sure, my lord, I did not mean to make any improper reflections on the way in which this prosecution had been conducted; and if your lordship had listened to me only until I had completed my sentence, you would not have considered the matter in the same point of view. Gentlemen, we have had, then, these drawings presented before us, and I hope at least, that they have been confined to this place; I hope they have not been exhibited out of Court, to influence the judgment, and inflame the passions of the public, and to influence, and to inflame your passions, as a part of the general community. I do not mean to insinuate for a moment, that my learned friend would descend to such a contrivance, he is the last man in the world, to pervert the designs of justice, by such dishonourable means.

"In addition to this, we have not only had the oral evidence of the witnesses, but we have had a sort of acting introduced. You have not forgotten, I am sure, the attitudes in which the gentleman on the floor placed himself, to all which I consented, that you might have every possible assistance in proceeding to your decision; and having concurred, it would be indeed unjustifiable, if I were to object to it, and all the use I wish to make of these remarks is, that you may now have present in your minds, the nature of the offence, with which this defendant is charged.

" What is the sort of punishment? My friend says, there is a mode of punishment in this country, called picquetting, but that this is a matter perfectly distinct, and availing himself of a sort of pun, on the name of the defendant, he tells you that this should be called Pictonning, and not Picquetting. What the distinction is between them, which recurs to the mind of my learned friend, I cannot at all discover; in both instances, whether applied to this young woman in Trinidad, or used in England as a military punishment, the picquet is the situation to which the foot is applied, and it requires more lights than I can avail myself of, to discern any difference between them. Without going deeply into the subject, let any of us resort to a common dictionary, and we shall find the explanation of picquetting, exactly and literally, an explanation of what was applied in this particular case.

" Now, gentlemen, let us pause for a moment, and not permit our feelings to be hurried onward, with a rapidity dangerous to the exercise of our deliberate judgment. We see that even in this country, where

we so justly boast of the humanity, of our laws, and
of the benign spirit of our national institutions, this
practice of picqueting, at which we should be taught
to start with horror by the eloquence of my friend,
actually prevails. And to whom is it directed? It
is, we have seen, used as a military punishment, that
is, employed against the meritorious class of men,
who are immediately engaged in the defence, and
who constantly maintain the glory of the empire.
| "Slight torture, then, known and practised in our own
land, was applied in the case of a capital offence;
and had this young person been convicted, she would,
under the mandate of our laws, have lost her
life. In other words, the defendant simply ordered
the application of a military punishment, on the suggestion of the magistrate, who was bound in the first
instance to enquire into the nature and circumstances
of the offence.

" Was this lawful or not by the law of Spain? I
readily agree with my friend, that torture was
not applied in England, and we are referred by
him to the learned author of the Commentaries on the
Law of England, whose work, with some few excep-
tions, may be considered as a fine and elegant illustration of the principles and practice of British law.
This writer tells us, as we have been reminded by my
learned friend, that ' upon the assassination of Villiers Duke of Buckingham by Felton, it was proposed
in the Privy Council to put the assassin to the rack,
in order to discover his accomplices; the judges, be-

ing consulted, declared unanimously, to their own honour, and the honour of the English law, that no such proceeding was allowable by the laws of England.' But my learned friend has forgotten in his application of this passage, that ' the honour of the English law' was here placed in advantageous comparison with the law of other countries; and that for the express purpose of the contradistinction, the ingenious commentator introduced this historical fact. And thus am I able to collect from the reading of my learned friend a most material illustration of the argument to which I am immediately directing your view, for, from Judge Blackstone, we are informed, that although torture is unknown here, yet that torture was the practice of other countries ; and to shew that this was the practice in the island of Trinidad, is the pursuit in which I am now engaged. If, then, I can make it evident to you, that by the instructions, received from Sir Ralph Abercrombie, the defendant was bound by the law of Spain, the question will not be, as my friend seemed to suppose, whether torture be a crime by the law of England, but if it be so by the law of Spain. And here I will premise that it seems to have been so notorious that such was the Spanish law, that the whole enquiry, as it has been hitherto conducted under the commission appointed, proceeds on the ground, that torture was permitted under the Spanish jurisdiction. A question is proposed, whether it is customary by the law of Spain, that the party suffering torture should have a defensor? The answer is in the affirmative; and you observe, both the interrogatory and the reply presume that torture was admitted by that law.

" In the progress of this enquiry it will appear, that a defensor was actually appointed in the particular stage of the business, when the law directed such a nomination.

" The object of torture is to compel a discovery; but it would be a mockery of the proceeding, to assign a defensor at the moment the torture was to be applied. What could his duty be in such a situation? He was not to determine if the torture should be inflicted; the judge did not need his permission for its exercise.

" Another question is proposed under the commission proceeding on the same presumptive enquiries, what is the nature, and what are the kinds of torture; and the answer explains the expedients by water, fire, and some of the various means used for the purpose. Thus, upon the very evidence prepared for your inspection in the long history of this cause, it will appear, that by the law of Spain torture was applicable to this particular case.

" Begorat says, that the modes of torture under particular offences are not distinguished by the law of Spain; that in this respect the matter is left to the discretion of the judge, and to the constitution of the patient.

" We have here to consider the mildest species of torture, much lighter than was usually applied in

Spain, and every witness that is called in succession to be interrogated, swears that torture is applicable to the case of evidence, and that it is so by the law of Spain, There was no Spanish lawyer to be resorted to on the island, and therefore on this question, recourse was had to the best authority, the nature of the case admitted of, and that was, to the Spanish law books, recognized, as containing the principles and practice of the law of this settlement.

" Then, here is the case of a young woman who is examined on the occasion of a capital offence being committed, it is found that she conceals the truth, and it appears, that the man with whom she held carnal intercourse (Carlos Gonzaler) committed the robbery constituting that capital offence.

" Permit me now to suppose, that the defendant had thought fit, previously to giving the order for slight torture, to have examined the Alcalde Begorat, as to the laws regulating its application. This criminal judge would have told the governor, that torture in such cases was conformable to the institutions of the Spanish law, and every other person conversant on the subject whom the defendant might think fit to have consulted, would have confirmed the same opinion. In addition to this, he would have been told, that it was not only an oral law, but that it was a written law, that there were books or treatises upon it which were constantly made use of in the colony over which he presided.

" Gentlemen of the Jury, I have the satisfaction to tell you that the very books to which this magistrate would have referred you, are now in court; I hold one of them at this moment in my hand, so that with the assistance of translators, you will have all the advantage of the illustrations they can give you on the tenor of the Spanish laws as referable to this case. I have examined them with much attention, and have discovered their immediate application to the subject. Are these, you will enquire, books of acknowledged authority? On this subject, we have availed ourselves of the knowledge and experience of the king's attorney general, Mr. Archibald Gloster, who will appear in the witness-box and inform you, that these are the books constantly resorted to on the island for legal information.

" The first of these I shall notice is the *Curia Philippica*. In folio 202 of that work, it is said, that the question or torture is to be applied when proof is deficient, and it is to be resorted to indifferently, both to witnesses or criminals, if they deny the truth. Folio 230, it says, that the question may be ordered to force a confession of accomplices; then it adds, that the torment cannot be directed, excepting in the instance of attrocious crimes; and it proceeds to some distinctions of cases where it is justifiable under all circumstances, and particularly, where persons having the care of property, a theft is committed of such property under their charge. And gentlemen, you will learn, that this case, where torture is expressly directed, is precisely that case which is now submitted to your observation.

" And now, let us consider for a moment what are the benefits necessarily resulting from this species of proof. This is not an explanation of the Spanish law by the oral testimony of witnesses who may be ignorant of its principles, and wholly unacquainted with its practice. Such witnesses might adapt their testimony to the immediate occasion to rescue a criminal from the vengeance of the British laws. These printed authorities are removed from all possibility of corruption, they are the ancient established law of the land, and are incapable of being suited by any artifice to the case of a particular individual. There is no variation in their testimony at different periods; they speak the same language they did when they first appeared before the world; they speak the same sentiments before you at this moment, and they will continue to do so, now, and for ever.

" Thus, gentlemen, whether we look to the evidence of the witnesses as it has been delivered in court, or whether we attend to the written proof as it appears in the enquiries under the commission, or in the volumes now before me, we shall find it unquestionably and universally laid down, that the officer possessing the supreme military and civil authority in the island of Trinidad, had it in his discretion to adminster torture.

" But not to detain you——"

LORD ELLENBOROUGH. (interposing) " Have you any precedents as to the mode, and the degree ?"

MR. DALLAS. "There is one as to the forms ; I

1

will produce the passage, but it has already appeared that the species of torment applicable to particular cases, is not prescribed by the law."

LORD ELLENBOROUGH. "Should not the judge have attended to the mode of its application? I am unwilling to interrupt you, but I do it in order that you may direct your attention usefully, to what may constitute the principal difficulty."

MR. DALLAS. "I am aware of your kind intentions, my lord, and I will apply my argument to what you have pointed out. The mode is distinguished; dropping of water, small cord and pullies, and punishments of that nature. The persons to be present are only the judge, the escribano, or secretary, the executioner, and the criminal. No other individual is even to be within hearing, and exactly as it was enacted by law, was the torture on this occasion applied.

" Having found, then, that the occasion on which the torture was applied, was precisely that pointed out in words by the law ; that the mode of its application was with the same strictness complied with, and that the persons present were those directed to attend by the same authority : the next question is, and the only one referable to this part of the case, whether the defendant was the proper judge to resort to, for the issue of the order which was the foundation of the whole proceeding ? This doubt, in the preceding observations, has been fully satisfied. It has been shewn that the ordinary judge could not

inflict the torture without the mandate of the defendant, and that no appeal was possible in a case of this
kind, because the power of the Audience of the Caraccas and of the royal Council of Madrid, had been
superseded by the conquest.

"To draw these remarks to a single point which
I submit to your view, with proper deference, under
the direction of the noble and learned judge, I
affirm, that whatever may be the principles of law, as
recognised by the law of England, that which is a
justification of the charge of this indictment in the
country where the act was committed, is a full and
complete vindication in this place.

"Gentlemen, I have already stated to you that the
charge not only alleges that he did the act unlawfully, but without motive or probable cause. Let
us examine this by steps. It is thus asserted, that it
was not only unlawful, but malicious. I have already
endeavoured to explain that an act may be unlawfully done, and erroneously done, without being
malicious or criminal : but no man can possibly do
that which is malicious without involving criminality
with the act; and, therefore, agreeably with the arrangement I have adopted, I have first enquired if
the proceeding were unlawful, and it is now incumbent on me to examine if it were malicious.

"Malice, gentlemen, is of two kinds, expressed,
and implied. The first is a principle of ill will operate towards the particular individual. It is commonly
the effect of an antecedent quarrel in a mind badly

regulated, or, it may be said to be, revenge lurking in the heart. In the sense to which we are now adverting, it is a design to infringe the laws of the land, and to carry this violation into execution when a favourable opportunity offers; and the evidence of this disposition, received in our courts, is of the nature of the act itself. Looking at the whole circumstances of this case, I can hardly entertain the smallest suspicion that you can suppose any express malice to exist in this case, and it appears to me, at least, that there is not a tittle of evidence to support such a conjecture."

LORD ELLENBOROUGH. "If it be unlawful, the act is presumed to be malicious. You will recollect a cause which came on respecting granting licenses, in which this matter was a good deal considered. This ground that you are now taking, may be extremely material in mitigation of punishment, but it does not go the length with regard to the verdict of guilty, or not guilty, which you seem inclined to suppose."

MR. GARROW. "My learned friend seems to me to endeavour to establish a distinction where there is no difference; when we state the intention to oppress, we mean merely to say that the act oppresses."

LORD ELLENBOROUGH. "There is certainly a distinction where malice is a distinction of law, and where malice is of the essence of the act."

I

Mr. Garrow. " But this reasoning does not apply to the simple question of the guilt or innocence of the defendant, although it may refer to the *quantum* of guilt."

Lord Ellenborough. "Malice is the colour of law, which applies to the act, and the law draws the inference."

Mr. Dallas. " I was about to state, my lord, simply this, that there was no evidence of express malice."

Lord Ellenborough. " It is not even pretended."

Mr. Dallas. " Then, gentlemen, I am permitted to say, from this high authority, that there is no express malice, and I am thus relieved from a difficulty with which the question might possibly have been attended. I understand it then to be said from the bench, that the averment, coupled with the word unlawful, is to be taken as one intire allegation, and that the malice is to be assumed as an inference of law."

Lord Ellenborough. " If the act be unlawful, it is a sufficient ground of conviction, although the party may have erroneously committed it."

Mr. Dallas. " His lordship has now ruled that we are to put out of our consideration all enquiries as to actual malice, and, if the act committed were unlawful, the illegality alone will be sufficient to render the defendant guilty."

LORD ELLENBOROUGH. " This is a case, Mr. Dallas, full of important points ; points of much more consequence than the last to which you have adverted; but if you have any authorities as to this particular, I shall be glad to hear them."

Mr. DALLAS. " In a well known case, my lord, Lord Chief Justice de Grey, took the distinction on which I am now insisting ; and the argument there proceeds upon such persons being civilly responsible, although not criminally, where they do that which is unlawful ignorantly. It seems to me that it is against the principles of natural justice, that a man should suffer criminally, for his ignorance of the law, but I have no difficulty in conceding that he should civilly."

LORD ELLENBOROUGH. " To say that no man is to be considered as criminal, because he was mistaken, would be leaving it to the artifice of a man not to inform himself, in order that he might not be considered criminal. The subject was much considered, when Mr. Justice Chambre was at the bar, and then it was held'; that although the defendant were mistaken, yet that his ignorance was no competent defence. It was a very good reason for mitigation of punishment, but no ground for his not being convicted."

Mr. DALLAS. "Getlemen, understanding the subject as I now do, I shall confine myself to the enquiry in this place, whether the torture was applicable by the law of Spain. But this question is necessarily

connected with another as applied to this defendant.
What was the situation of General Picton? In the
reply to this interrogatory, I am to maintain that
his situation does furnish an answer to the charge
in the indictment. I say it does upon this ground:
The defendant, as governor, was supreme criminal judge, and it appears, that what he did was
done by him in the course of regular judicial enquiry. Sustaining this character, he hears the report which is made to him according to the established forms, and he gives the order on which the
charge is founded.

"The first point to examine is, if he were
cloathed with that sort of judicial authority, which
brings him within the protection of the law. I do
not mean to assert that his person was enfolded
within the robes, and that he was attended by all
the insignia of justice; but I contend that he was
armed with the full powers, so as to afford him all
the protection that the law of England provides
for such high officers. Your lordship will recollect that Lord Mansfield was very explicit on this
subject, and I can have no difficulty in arguing
that this defendant, placed in a foreign settlement
is within the reason of the rule, which supplies protection to a judge of record. I will presently enquire into one or two authorities in support of my
position. It is laid down, that no one, in such a
situation, is liable to prosecution for what they do
in the course of their judicial functions, in your

situation, my lord, it would be a sufficient answer to a charge were you to say, "True it is, I did it maliciously, but I did it serving in my character as a judge." Still more removed from any penal consequence, must it be, if it were done erroneously, and not maliciously. In the 1 *Hawkins*, 309, also jurors are exempted from penal consequences for what they do in their character of jurors, although in the ordinary."

Lord Ellenborough (interposing). "I take the distinction to be this: if a judge in the ordinary exercise of his jurisdiction commits an error, the law will not allow, that he should be prosecuted criminally: but if he commits an error out of such jurisdiction, he is then liable."

Mr. Dallas. "I am well aware of this necessary, and important distinction, to which I was proceeding; and as protection applies to those cases, when they are in the ordinary exercise of juridical powers, and while so employed, although they act maliciously, still they will receive the same protection. With regard to what are considered in law, the limits of their jurisdiction, I can bring to your Lordship's recollection, a strong case of that kind."

Lord Ellenborough. "I think there are many points in this case, which make it fit, that it should be turned into a special verdict. There are several matters connected with the Spanish law, that require particular examination."

MR. GARROW. " My lord, I can have no objection whatever to such a proposition."

LORD ELLENBOROUGH. " Sitting at Guildhall, if they were proving the existence of a certain law, and such law were in writing, it would be required that they should have a copy of the law."

MR. GARROW. " I should be sorry, my lord, if, entrusted with the conduct of a prosecution, of such great importance, I could be capable of throwing difficulties in their way, to prevent the discovery of the truth. They have now the opportunity to prove the existence of the laws, for which they contend by the books before them, and I shall not object, if these should be deficient, to admit them to give oral evidence on the subject."

LORD ELLENBOROUGH. " For the purpose we have in view, the law must not remain doubtful; we must take the law either one way, or the other. I observe then that if the counsel for the prosecution think that the matter in question is reasonably made out, to be the law of Spain, it will be allowed to be so stated."

MR. GARROW. " Yes, my Lord, if there s reasonable evidence of the existence of such law, I shall give my consent to its being so stated."

LORD ELLENBOROUGH. " I should be disposed to go further, and to say that text writers, of high reputation, I would take to be accurate expounders of the law, for the purpose of this verdict. The

counsel for the defendant may now proceed with
his evidence, and pray a special verdict."

Mr. GARROW. " I shall with great confidence
contend, that whatever may be the law of Spain,
no light in which it can appear, will operate in
favour of the defendant, and if I am correct in
this, then they may take the law of Spain to be
what they please."

LORD ELLENBOROUGH. " That will be open for
you to argue, with the various other points of the
cause."

MR. DALLAS. " Gentlemen, from the conver-
sation which has now taken place, I find my task is nearly at
an end, therefore, I shall detain you
no longer in discussing the facts which are to appear on the special verdict: if there be, or be
not a justification in point of law, will be a matter of future enquiry.

" In proceeding to the proofs, we shall endeavour to adopt some arrangement, so as to relieve
you as much as possible, from unnecessary mental exertion.

" We shall first put in the instructions from
Sir Ralph Abercrombie to the defendant. We
have the Gazette here in which the capitulation is
contained. After the instructions of the officer,
by whom the conquest was effected, we shall give
his Majesty's instructions, which succeeded in order of time."

Evidence for the defendant.

The London Gazette was put in, dated the 27th of March, 1797, containing the articles of capitulation, on the surrender of the island of Trinidad.

The instructions from Sir Ralph Abercrombie were also put in, and the titles read, whereby it appeared that the defendant was appointed Commander of Trinidad.

LORD ELLENBOROUGH. " You should shew that the law of Spain prevailed in the colony prior to the capitulation."

MR. GARROW. " I cannot admit generally, that the law of Spain obtained; I may admit that the law of Spain obtained under certain qualifications."

LORD ELLENBOROUGH. " Then you will shew the qualifications."

MR. GARROW. " I conceive that this task will not devolve upon me, for when the law of Spain is produced as it existed in the colony, it will be shewn to be a qualified law. We should say generally, that Jamaica was governed by the laws of England, and yet it would not be accurate to assert, that the two islands were governed by the same laws. So perhaps it may be said generally, that Trinidad was governed by the law of Spain, but on a nearer inspection of the law, as it prevailed in Trinidad, it would be discovered that qualifications were introduced, and that the law which subsisted there, was much milder than that which prevailed in Spain."

2

MR. LAWES, (on the part of the defendant) " We know of no particular code framed for the island of Trinidad, or generally for the colonial dependencies of Spain, and, therefore, are bound only by the law as promulgated in the parent state."

LORD ELLENBOROUGH. "First the *onus* is upon them to shew what particular law prevailed. This is the first step, and then, until the contrary be proved, the presumption will be in favour of the date of the country to which the island belonged."

MR. GARROW. "Yes, according to the rule your Lordship has laid down, if by the authority of a text writer they can establish that the law of Spain prevailed."

LORD ELLENBOROUGH. " Very likely, they will give parol evidence as to this particular."

MR. DALLAS. " Unfortunately, my Lord, Mr. Gloster, the Attorney General, went to the island long after the capitulation. The evidence we give is, that Trinidad was a Spanish Colony, and from that single fact, the presumption is, that it is governed by the Spanish law. I know of no particular code such as that to which my learned friend seems to have so frequently referred."

LORD ELLENBOROUGH. " You must in the first instance, give some probable evidence as to the law, and if you do not go at least thus far, we cannot proceed with any regularity."

MR. DALLAS. " My Lord, I have put in the instructions under which the defendant acted, and these all refer to the Spanish law :—the laws of the colony, used under the Spanish government.

MR. GARROW. "In answer to this, my Lord, I have a document in the defendant's own hand writing, in which he says, that Trinidad is not governed by the law of old Spain, but according to the laws of the Indies, and these laws being corrected, and highly improved, are considered a perfect code of colonial government ; he distinctly remarks that the colony is not governed by the law of Spain."

MR. DALLAS. "I have not seen or heard of the paper to which my learned friend refers and therefore can give no answer to it."

MR. GARROW. "He goes on to say, that this island was exempted from the general principle of colonial government, in order to increase the population of it. There is a special code, and the references made, are not to the laws of old Spain, but to those of the Indies."

LORD ELLENBOROUGH. "You are to shew the existence of some law, and to make your way to it in the best manner you can. (To Mr. Dallas.)

MR. DALLAS. "The regular way would be, for us to go through our proof, and then it will be seen what it amounts to."

LORD ELLENBOROUGH. "I wish you to say distinctly where it is deficient, for I am afraid without some admission on the part of the prosecution, you will not be able to proceed. If what the defendant has done be not under the authority of law, he ought to he punished ; if under that authority, he ought to be quit and go free, however repugnant this might be to our feelings."

Mr. Dallas. "For the purpose of shewing that it was under that authority, I will produce some passage from the exhibits.

"The exhibit F says, that in criminal causes, reference shall be had to the governor, and that no sentence shall be executed until it is approved by him. It proceeds, no capitulation having been made in this island, for continuing the Spanish form of law, and that form of law being continued only by my circular letters to Magistrates, in order to avoid the confusion which may arise from the strict adherence to that form of law under the English government, directions will be given you in your instructions from General Picton, to explain my meaning and intentions fully in this particular. And whereas, I have thought proper to remove from his office &c. the assessor, I direct you to proceed in all criminal cases without an assessor, however contrary it may be to the Spanish forms of law; and all sentences signed by you without an assessor, shall be as good and valid, &c."

The instructions from England to Thomas Picton governor and commander in chief over the Island of Trinidad, dated St. James's, 1st of June, 1801, were now read. The fifth article says.

"It is our will, that the present administration should be exercised by you according to the terms hereunto annexed, and according to the ancient

laws and institutions previously to the surrender of
the island, as nearly as may be, subject to such direction, as you shall now, or hereafter receive from
us, &c.

"The seventh article directs, that the powers to
be exercised by the English governor, are such as
were before intrusted to the Spanish governor.

The commission from his Majesty to the defendant was then delivered. It was dated on the
1st of June, 1801, in the 41st year of the king."

MR. LAWES. "We put in this, my Lord, merely
that your Lordship may make a memorandum of
its production."

LORD ELLENBOROUGH. "You must prove what
is the description of an Alcalde."

MR. DALLAS. "We have witnesses to that, my
Lord. We are now upon the Spanish law, the rule
of conduct. I think it will be better first to call
witnesses to prove the nature of the office, and
then to produce other evidence, as to the law of
the colony. It would be more expedient for us,
to proceed with the parol evidence, before we bring
forward the documentary. Surely we shall not
now read the evidence which occupied 11 days; it
will only be necessary to refer to the commission of
General Picton."

LORD ELLENBOROUGH. "That has nothing to
do with the question."

MR. LAWES. "It is evidence that the defendant
acted in his judicial capacity."

LORD ELLENBOROUGH. " It can neither preju-
dice or benefit his case in any way. There can
be no doubt however, of his holding the rank of
Alcalde. In this stage of the cause, you give evidence of what was communicated. At any rate
General Picton ordered Gonzalez to be discharged
and banished from the Island."

MR. GARROW. " I have no objection to its being
taken in that way."

M. Michael Gourville was then called and
examined by Mr. Lawes, assisted by an interpreter.

Q. When did you first go to the Island of Trinidad? A. In the year 1774.

Q. How long did you remain there? A. Until
I came to this country about two months ago.

Q. Who was governor when first you went
there? A. Don Manuel Falques.

Q. When did M. Chapon become governor of
the Island? A. He was governor 11 years.

Q. Did you act in the character of Alcalde
and of what class? A. I was Alcalde for one
year.

Q. Under whose government? A. M. Chapon's.

Q. Were there different classes of Alcaldes, or
only one? A. There was a first, and second class,
but the jurisdiction was the same.

Q. Had the governor the like jurisdiction with
the Alcaldes? A. Equal with them.

Q. Did they both act as judges, or was the sentence of the one appealed to from the other?

A. they appealed in criminal cases to the Royal audience of the Caraccas.

Q. How was the sentence executed, and on what authority? A. By the authority of the judges themselves, and every thing belonging to the police was under the same authority."

LORD ELLENBOROUGH. "The witness must be mistaken, he said, in criminal cases they appealed to the Caraccas."

MR. DALLAS. "The witness says, my lord, that mere matters of police were decided in the island."

MR. GARROW. "You appear to have selected this interpreter for his unfitness."

Question, by MR DALLAS. Could not the sentence for any offence he executed in the island?

The interpreter not being able to make the witness comprehend the interrogation, and his lordship not thinking him competent to the duty, another was sent for, and, upon his arrival, the following questions were put to M. Gourville, under the direction of Mr. Lawes,

Q. Could the Alcalde, or the Governor, pronounce sentence upon prisoners without an assessor? A. They can, but they are responsible when they are not attended by a man of the law.

MR. GARROW. "This answer, my lord, is that they might do such a thing but they would be responsible."

INTERPRETER "He said they did do it, but, unless they were attended by a man of the law, they were responsible."

Q. By what authority were their sentences at last executed? The witness did not understand the question.

Q. Were the sentences referred to the court of Caraccas? A. I do not know if they appeal now; but, at the time General Picton was governor, it was impossible.

Q. We are not asking concerning that transaction, but was it so at the time Chapon was governor? A. The appeal was always to the audience of Caraccas.

Q. Do you know how sentences were enforced when the appeal to Caraccas ceased? A. I had only to do with the affairs at the time of the appeals. I saw Governor Picton inflict punishments of different natures, but, at the time of the government of M. Chapon, I only saw persons flogged.

MR. GARROW. "He says he saw them only whipped, my lord."

Q. In what cases was flogging inflicted? A. In robbery in the streets, violence to women, &c."

LORD ELLENBOROUGH. "You can refer us to the law upon the subject. The governor does not appear to have interfered in the first instance. There seems to be no subordinate authority. The interpreter and the witness must be both wrong."

Mr. Dallas, " Neither interfered with the other in matters of police; but, in cases of life and death, appeals were made to the royal audience of Caraccas"

Lord Ellenborough. " It looks as if they had concurrent jurisdictions."

Q. How were the sentences pronounced by the Alcalde, or the Governor?

Mr. Garrow. " It was quite impossible to suppose that the governor was to perform the office of both Jack Ketch an executioner."

Lord Ellenborough. " It is a thing impossible to be imagined."

Q. Was there a person called an assessor? A. Yes, there was a man of the law, called either an assessor, or an auditor."

Q. What was the office of the man of the law called the auditor? A. He was obliged to attend the judge in all cases, and give his opinion to the Governor, or Alcalde.

Q. Was this before the conquest of Trinidad, or both before and after? A. Both before and after.

Q. What was the duty of the Escribano. A. He was to take notes of all that was done.

Q. What is the difference between a Judge Laico, and a Judge Imperito? A. A Judge Laico is a person established in that office by law, I should suppose.

Q. What was a Judge Laico, was he a lawyer or not? A. The Alcaldes are not necessarily men ac-

2

quainted with the law, they are elected from the mass of the inhabitants.

MR. DALLAS. "I fancy, my lord, a Judge Laico must mean a lay Judge."

Q. When they are not men of the law, are they called Judges Laico's? A. They are chosen by election.

MR. GARROW. "The fact is, my lord, there is no such distinction as my friends are endeavouring to establish."

Q. Are there any other judges but Alcaldes? The witness, not understanding the question, answered that the Alcaldes were chosen from the inhabitants.

Q. Are lawyers or laymen elected? A. There is no necessity for their being lawyers."

Q. If the Alcalde be not a man of the law, who acts as his assessor? A. If he have no assessor, he decides according to his conscience.

LORD ELLENBOROUGH. "This must be subsequent to the time of the capture by Sir Ralph Abercrombie, because, by the old government, they had this man of the law. I cannot take this to be the positive law of the country."

Q. When do you first remember a lawyer in the country? Q. At the arrival of M. Chapon there were several.

LORD ELLENBOROUGH: "You are speaking of Governor Picton's time."

Q. Do you remember the time when Mr. Justice Nihil, was removed? A. He was removed five years ago, about a year after the surrender.

Q. Was there any chief justice, or office of that nature in the Island till after the conquest.

Lord Ellenborough. "I have understood him to say that in the time of the Spanish government, there were no judges but Alcaldes.

Q. Has any other person been appointed chief justice, since the removal of Mr. Nihil.

Lord Ellenborough. "What was his description?"

Mr. Garrow. "He was appointed chief justice to the Island of Trinidad, during His Majesty's pleasure.

Q. Has any body been appointed to the place since the removal of Mr. Nihil?

Mr. Garrow. "You must not assume Mr. Lawes that he has been removed, in the absence of proof to support it."

Q. Has any body been appointed in Mr. Nihil's place? A. No.

Q. Has Mr. Nihil been in any other court or place since, and in what?

Mr. Garrow. "I must object, my Lord."

Q. When did Nihil cease to act as chief justice? A. I was in England and knew nothing about it.

Q. There have been no judges for some time? A. Yes, there were persons who divided matters.

Q. Who acted as judge there? A. A judge was appointed by the general.

Q. Who was the judge, and when was the defendant made governor? A. Mr. Nihil.

Q. Who was appointed judge of the Consulado? A. Mr. Nihil.

LORD ELLENBOROUGH. "What are we about? You are trifling with the court in putting such questions. We are now examining who is the criminal: it is really abusing the privilege of the special verdict, and when we are at considerable pains to collect materials, we are pestered with the Consulado."

The Witness cross-examined, by Mr. Garrow.

Q. Did not Mr. Nihil continue in the Island till you came away? A. Yes he did.

Q. Did he not continue to act as chief justice until you came away? A. He was judge of the Consulado.

Q. Did he not remain judge in the same manner as he had done at the beginning. A. I believe not.

Q. Why did he not? A. Because he was named only to the Consulado.

Q. Before the nomination, did the governor in the first instance interfere with respect to prisoners and witnesses?

MR. GOURVILLE not being able to comprehend the interpreter, Colonel De Chabilier tendered his services in that office, which were accepted with thanks by his Lordship.

Q. Before the nomination, did the governor in the first instance interfere with respect to prisoners, and witnesses? A. No, he never interfered in the first instance before the Alcalde, because the party who complained had always a right to select his own judge.

Q. Were there at that time two Alcaldes? A. Yes, two.

Q. The party, you say, who complained had always a right to go before whom he pleased had he not? or if he liked he might chuse the governor? A. Yes.

Q. If he chose the Alcalde, did the governor interfere? A. No, the governor did not intermeddle.

Q. I am speaking of cases of a criminal nature? A. There was no interference in either case.

Q. Did you ever know an instance, in the time of M. Chapon, of torture being applied? A. Never.

Q. Was it ever applied to those accused, or suspected of any criminal affair? A. Never.

Q. Before the arrival of Governor Picton, was there any instrument for its infliction? A. I never had any knowledge of it.

Q. If there had been, must you have known it? A. I think I must: but sometimes they tied the thumbs of criminals together.

Q. Did you during the year you were in office attend the goals; and did you see any instruments of torture? A. I did attend, but I observed none.

Q. Do you know the room in which the torture, was applied to Louisa Calderon? A. No.

LORD ELLENBOROUGH. There is evidence, that no instrument of torture was applied, or even, in existence, till after the arrival of the defendant.

Q. Did you ever know any instance of tying the thumbs of witnesses together? A. No, never.

In what cases of criminality, did they tie the thumbs? A. Of people who have robbed, and committed petty offences.

Q. Do you recollect the first instrument of torture, used by Governor Picton? A. I was then in this country.

Q. Did you ever know the circumstance of tying the thumbs of slaves.

LORD ELLENBOROUGH. "That goes only to shew that there existed such a law in Spain, Mr. Dallas you had better address yourself to the law of the Colony the case is left by this testimony just where it was."

MR. GARROW. "There is no reason in the world for supposing, that the judges interfered in the first instance.

MR. JOHN NUGENT was then called and examined by Mr. Dallas.

Q. How long had you been in Trinidad, before the arrival of General Picton? A. I went there in the year 1786, and came away in 1797, making a stay of 11 years.

Q. During the whole course of that time, in what manner was criminal justice administered? A. There are three courts. That of the governor, and the two Alcaldes, which are of equal, and concurrent authority.

Q. In the case of a charge of theft, before whom did the trial take place? A. Before either one of them; before any one of the three.

Q. Supposing the party to have been found guilty of theft, what happened then? A. Then the sentence, was transmitted to the Royal Audiance of the Caraccas, for its confirmation, or rejection.

Q. Then the appeal was not from one court to the other, on the island, but to the Caraccas? A. That was the appeal.

Q. But the conviction took place before each seperate judge, and was transmitted with the proceedings, to the audience of the Caraccas? A. Yes, and in some instances, with the person of the prisoner so convicted.

Q. What was the distinction between the Judge, Laico, and Imperito? A. The Judge, Laico, is elected from the ordinary merchants, or planters, and is chosen by the Cabildo. *

* Cabildo from the Latin Capitulum. It is a chapter of a Church; also a Common Council, or a Court of Aldermen of a tonw—Pineda.

Lord Ellenborough. Q. "What is the Cabildo?" A. I take it my Lord to be something like the Lord Mayor and Aldermen of the city of London, with greater authority. They have very considerable privileges, and are called the illustrious Cabildo. It is chosen by a majority of votes.

Q. Is the Alcalde a lawyer, or chosen indiscriminately? A. He is chosen from the mass of the inhabitants.

Q. What is the Judge Imperito? * A. I conceive it to be the auditor. I do not know the term, I never heard it before. The only distinction I ever was acquainted with, was the Alcalde.

Q. In some cases the party appealed, did he not? A. Yes, and then the proceedings were laid before the Royal Audience of Caraccas, before sentence was passed, or carried into execution.

Q. Was there an appeal from the Caraccas, to the King, and Council at Madrid? A. Yes, there was.

Q. During the Spanish government, had not the Alcaldes, the assistance of an assessor, appointed by the governor? A. They had, and during the English administration, the clerk was appointed assessor.

Q. When did you leave the Island? A. I quitted it in July, 1802.

Q. Had Mr. Nihil, before that time, ceased to act as criminal Judge? A. I do not know if he executed the office.

* Imperito from the Latin, and means as in the original language, unskilful.—

Q. Was he called Criminal Judge? A. Yes, he was.

Q. What was he at the time of the conquest? A. He was an Alcalde, but was appointed Chief Justice, by Sir Ralph Abercrombie, and was consulted in his official capacity.

Q. Do you know that he exercised criminal Judicature? A. No, I do not.

Q. In what capacity had he acted, for some time previous to your quitting the Island? A. He had acted under the commission of Sir Ralph Abercrombie.

" LORD ELLENBOROUGH. " How do you apply this to the present case? The Governor authorised the infliction of torture. Mr. Nihil appears to have nothing to do with it, either in a civil, or criminal point of view. Governor Picton, took upon himself, to authorise the proceeding, and to inflict torture, as you say, agreeably to the laws of Spain."

The witness cross-examined by Mr. Adam.

Q. How long had you been in the Island before the conquest? A. From 1797, to 1802; five years.

Q. Did you ever see the torture administered, or hear of its being inflicted in any case? A. No, I never did.

Q. Was there any instrument of torture, introduced by the laws o Spain? A. I cannot tell, but I think not, unless it were after I quitted the Island.

Q. Do you mean to say, that you do not know if the torture was inflicted?

THE WITNESS. "My Lord, the gentlemen seems to wish to embarrass me, I am very weak, and throw myself upon your Lordship's protection."

LORD ELLENBOROUGH. "I assure you, Mr. Nugent, you totally misunderstand; Mr. Adam is only asking concerning a fact."

Q. By LORD ELLENBOROUGH. Have you ever known witnesses, that have had the torture inflicted?

MR. GARROW. "We will prove, my lord, that there were no instances of it."

LORD ELLENBOROUGH. "You have done enough to throw it upon them to prove it."

Mr. Archibald Gloster was then called, and examined by Mr. Dallas.

Q. How long, Sir, have you resided in the island of Trinidad? A. Since the 3d of June, 1803.

Q. What situation do you hold there? A. I have been his Majesty's Attorney General, since the 15th of October, when my warrant was signed. I am likewise a member of his Majesty's Council in the Island.

Q. I believe, Sir, you are acquainted with the different books of authority, used in Trinidad? A. I think I am.

Q. You mean to say you are acquainted with them? A. I have had reference to Spanish law books, and have had them brought before me, and stated to be authority.

M

Q. The Council of which you are a member, have acted upon them, have they not? A. Yes they have.

Mr. Garrow. "This proof, my lord, cannot be let in. Mr. Gloster had certain books laid before him, upon which he acted."

Lord Ellenborough. "He says he adopted them as legal authorities, and that they were acted upon in the administration of the laws."

Mr. Garrow. "If the witness had been asked, if he considered them the law of England? he might answer in the affirmative with as much reason."

Q. You have looked at the books? A. I have seldom inspected them.

Q. You have seen them I presume in your official situation? A. Yes I have.

Q. You are acquainted with the Bobadilla? A. Yes, I have seen it lying upon the table before the Council. It is a practical book.

Q. You likewise know the Elisondo, and the Curia Philippica? A. Yes, I have seen them also.

Q. In any case where a point was referred for the decision of the Council, were not the authorities annexed to it? A. No, the authorities were not affixed."

The Witness cross-examined by Mr. Harrison.

Q. Are you skilled or versed in the laws of Spain? A. No, I am not: I do not affect to know more than by reference to the books.

Q. Have you read the several books you state to

be authority? A. No, I have not; I have only dipped into them, and not studied them as if I intended to practise by them.

Q. Are they translated into English? A. No, they are not.

Q. Are you acquainted with the Spanish language? A. No, I am not; I can read it with a dictionary; and I have translated some passages.

Q. Then you are obliged to use a dictionary? A. Yes, I am, when I wish to read any parts.

Q. Do you not know that there is an authority exclusively applicable to the regulation of the colonies.

Q. By Mr. Garrow. A declaration of his Catholic Majesty respecting the laws of the island of Trinidad, entitled ‘ The Royal Schedula of his Majesty the King of Spain, containing rules for the population and commerce of the island of Trinidad? A. I believe there is such a book.

Q. And another book, called Recopilacion de Leyes, respecting the laws of the Indies, entitled “ Royal Letters and Orders ?” A. Yes, there is; and I know them to be books which are looked upon as authority.

Q. Is there a syllable in them which justifies the infliction of toture? A. I do not know that there is.

Q. You have not read them you say; these are the books used as the laws of the island?

Mr. Garrow. Q. Regulating the law of the colony in the present state? A. Yes.

Q. Where cases are of the greatest importance it was referred to the Court of Madrid; was it not? A. Yes, it was.

Question by LORD ELLENBOROUGH. Is there any law which regulates the manner of treating witnesses, who are contumaceous, or who prevaricate? A. I am aware of none in that book.

Q. How long have you been in the island? A. Since the year 1803.

LORD ELLENBOROUGH. "Mr. Dallas, you do not found yourself upon these books, do you?"

MR. DALLAS. "No, my lord. We shall now put in the books which have been mentioned, and read extracts from them. We may take them from the depositions."

LORD ELLENBOROUGH. "If you please."

MR. DALLAS. "The gentlemen on the other side may take the original, and if they find the translation incorrect, they may mention it."

LORD ELLENBOROUGH. "There must be an interpreter present, to check the depositions."

MR. GARROW. "We should be careful what is read, for I understand the greatest part of these authorities are commentaries on the law, and not the law itself."

An interpreter having taken the original, the title of the Curea Philippica was read in the following form:

"A Code of Laws, in a first and second volume.—The first, divided into five parts, wherein is briefly and compendiously treated, decisions in the

civil, criminal, ecclesiastical, and secular judica-
tures: with the determinations and opinions of
lawyers; useful for judges and advocates.—The
second volume divided into two parts, and three
books, wherein is treated the affairs of commerce
and inland government useful to merchants and
professors of jurisprudence."

The following passage was read from folio 229.

"Torment is inflicted to obtain the truth, not
having complete proof of it: for if there be proof,
it cannot be inflicted."

In the same page was contained the following
passage:

"In a similar crime to which the question is applicable to the delinquent, in the same it is applicable to the witness who varies and prevaricates in his
evidence, or who denies the truth, or who refuses
to declare it, there being presumption that he
knows it; not being to those persons to whom torment cannot be inflicted agreeably to any particular law."

Mr. Garrow. "That is the law laid down in
Partidas, with a Gregorian glossary, which says:

"And for the same crimes in which torment is
applicable to the delinquent, in case evidence of
evil character and bad morals is admitted, the witness is to testify under torment, if not, his evidence
is of no validity, agreeably to the laws of Partidas."

Folio 230 of the same book:

"The torment that may be ordered to the delin-

quent for the crime, may also be ordered to force
a declaration from the accomplices, and may also
be inflicted to oblige them to declare their accomplices, when there is a presumption, that such accomplices exist. The crimes of treason, both human and divine, unnatural offences, robbery, and
all others which probably cannot be committed without accomplices, which said accomplices may be
admitted as witnesses, as is determined in this case
by one Antonio Gonez."

The next passage read, was :

" The punishment to be according to the tempe-
rament of the delinquent, the crime and the presumption. New torments are not to be adopted, but
only the usual ones. The customary species of torture are those of water, small cords, a hook, or pulley, according to the Leys de las Partidas, and
therein it is mentioned by Gregorio de Lopez."

MR. DALLAS. " Now read the extract from the
same book, folio 291."

" There are to be present during the infliction
of torture only the judge, the notary, the executioner, and the party to be tormented. The torture is to be undergone in a place apart, and without
any other persons being within hearing."

MR. DALLAS. " These, my lord, are all the extracts I propose to make from the Curea Philippica ;
the next will be made from the book entitled Bobadilla.

LORD ELLENBOROUGH. " It should be understood, that the books are to be produced, and that the counsel for the prosecution should be at liberty to examine them at the proper time."

Mr. Dallas. "Certainly, my Lord."

Extract from the Bobadilla f. 964, No. 22:—"In the crime of high treason, manslaughter, robbery, parricide, and in other most attrocious crimes, should the presumption be strong, and the guilty person hardened, the lawyers say, that new tortures may be inflicted, but for this, the judges are to be responsible."

Lord Ellenborough. "There is no appearance of any thing like a regular law here."

Mr. Dallas. "Turn to page 965."

"Although during the infliction of torment judicially, the culprit should die, or should come out maimed therefrom, yet the judge neither can or ought to be blamed on that account, agreeable to the general opinion in the Leye de las Partidas wherein these words are employed. If the judge should put any man in torture for any crime he may have committed in order to ascertain the truth, he shall not be bound to make amends for the wounds he may occasion, and I well remember, that in the prison of this court, their died an assassin under torture, or from the result of it, and a leg was broken of another and no further notice taken of it."

Mr. Dallas. "Look at folio 962, No. 16."

" In notorious crimes, and most secretly transacted, against the most iniquitous men and of bad morals, if the judges order the torment, should witnesses be not quite sufficient—[Iuterpreter stopped. He afterwards proceeded.]   Although it is asserted that Paris de Putes says 'the use of the torture is only allowed to superior, and not inferior, judges, yet I know the practice is the contrary, and that for twenty-one years."

LORD ELLENBOROUGH   "This is too disputable to found the law upon, and it does not carry it at all farther.   I have struck it out from my notes."

MR. DALLAS. "Now proceed to folio 959, No. 10."

"If the crime be of a very serious nature, and the accused be a prisoner, he may not only be put in irons, but into the stocks and chains."

LORD ELLENBOROUGH. "This is quite remote from the subject; we are directing our attention wide of the mark."

MR. GARROW. "My lord, the book itself is only received upon the evidence of a man who cannot understand it, and who cannot make out a word of it without the assistance of a dictionary."

MR. DALLAS. "The next authority I shall produce is the Colom, and the passage is selected from the first volume, page 231."

"It is the part of the professional, or graduated lawyer, to determine the appearances which are sufficient to authorise torment.   But the question cannot be ordered by the ordinary judge, without consulting the superior tribunal."

Mr. Archibald Gloster was now recalled, who said that he did not know who Colom was. On examination by Mr. Lawes he added that he could not say if Colom were a book of authority in the island of Trinidad, but he thought he had seen it in the Escribano's office.

Lord Ellenborough. " There should be somebody accrediting the book, as of some acceptation in the country."

Mr. Dallas. " It appears to have been printed in 1795, at Madrid, *cum privilegio*."

Mr. Garrow. " The author is what I supposed, an Escribano, and is instructing his brethren."

Mr. Lawes. " It is a book like Impey's Practice, which is well received.

Mr. Dallas. " I should rather think it was a book in use."

Lord Ellenborough. Q. Mr. Gloster, you saw it on the island, did you not? A. Yes, my lord, I think I did.

Lord Ellenborough. " Then I think it stands on the same footing as the others."

Mr. Dallas. " We are under particular difficulty on account of the present situation of the two countries."

Lord Ellenborough. " I think you may read the book with all its imperfections: I will take down what is material."

Q. To Mr. Gloster, by Mr. Dallas. Is the Elisondo a book of practice? A. I believe it is.

Mr. Dallas. " The extract we purpose reading, my lord, is in page 273."

The interpreter not being present:

Lord Ellenborough.   Q. Mr. Gloster, can you translate the passage ?   A. No, my lord, I cannot, there are so many legal terms in it."

Mr. Garrow. " We should have thought, for that very reason, that you could have done it best."

The translator being returned, it was read in the following terms:

" A petition requesting torment to be inflicted on the ground of defective, proof T. in the name of R. in the cause that, in my behalf, is prosecuted against D. for this, that, and the other, I declare that the proofs for evidence being seen by your honour, brought forward in my behalf, that you will be pleased to order an infliction of torture on the said D. it being but justice, and, by carrying into execution, a favourable result may happen."

Mr. Dallas. " We shall now proceed, my lord, to the documentary evidence."

The first act of Begorat was then put in, dated in 1801. It was entitled:

" In a criminal cause, respecting the theft of two thousand hard dollars from Pedro Ruiz, before Don Aliero Begorat, ordinary judge at the port of Spain."

It then proceeded:

" At 6 o'clock, on the 5th of December, 1801, Pedro Ruiz was robbed of two thousand hard dollars, his trunk being broken open, and one of the planks of his chamber being forced away; and, therefore, the said Ruiz procured Louisa Calderon, her mother, and Carlos Gonzalez, to be arrested and brought before me, and I gave orders for the examination of witnesses, and the nearest neighbours, all which was communicated to the Governor; Louisa Calderon being committed."

MR. DALLAS. " We intend to take depositions, in their numbers, and then they may be inserted in their order in the special verdict."

MR. GARROW. " It does not appear that the circumstances of the robbery were communicated to the defendant, or that he acted upon them."

MR. LAWES. " Begorat's act proves they were laid before the General."

LORD ELLENBOROUGH. " It proved that something was laid before the defendant, but not that the individual proceedings were laid before him. Somebody should take the original, and observe if the translation be correct. Where do you find the signature of the General."

MR. GARROW. " In the order for inflicting the torture."

MR. DALLAS. " We now mean to read the depositions down to Number 11."

MR. GARROW. " I think I shall be saving your lordship's time, by stating this. They propose to read the depositions to shew that there was a strong suspicion that Louisa Calderon was concerned in the theft. I have no objection to take it in that way, as it certainly does appear, from the whole of the depositions, that there was a good ground for it."

LORD ELLENBOROUGH. " What deposition do you read now ?"

MR. DALLAS. " The evidence of Farfan, my lord."

MR. GARROW. " If they exclude from the special verdict any thing which we may think necessary to be introduced, I suppose we shall be at liberty to do it ?"

LORD ELLENBOROUGH. " Yes, certainly: but there must be this guard, not to put in any thing which is not admissible."

MR. GARROW. " There is, my lord, a great part of the depositions which are nothing like evidence."

LORD ELLENBOROUGH. " We must trust to its being excluded, or the special verdict may be sent back to be corrected."

MR. GARROW. " You will have the goodness to let us use your notes."

LORD ELLENBOROUGH. " Certainly ; they shall be at the service of the parties."

MR. DALLAS. " I believe we have nothing farther to trouble your lordship with."

LORD ELLENBOROUGH. " Then I will make a note that any of the depositions, or documents, which are legal evidence, are to be inserted in the special verdict, for either party requiring it. When I say evidence, I mean such as is admissible, and then I can refer to my notes."

MR. GARROW. " I propose calling witnesses to shew that torture is never applied by the old laws, as appears on the Recopilacion."

LORD ELLENBOROUGH. " Where the Recopilacion is silent, you may import something from Spain. The question is if they believe this evidence is contradicted by Gloster?"

MR. GARROW. " I doubt if Mr. Gloster's knowledge reaches as far as 1803."

LORD ELLENBOROUGH. "This appointment is in 1802; but his arrival in Trinidad is in 1803. The 15th of October, 1802, is the date of his warrant."

MR. GARROW. " We may ask him if he knew of the existence of the books at the time the punishment was inflicted."

Mr. Gloster recalled.

Q. When did you first arrive in Trinidad? A. On the 3d of January, 1803.

Q. Did you know of the existence of the books of authority you have mentioned before that time? A. No, I did not, I knew very little about them."

LORD ELLENBOROUGH. " He knows nothing about them."

MR. GARROW. " Neither inside or outside, I think, my lord."

Don Pedro de Vargas called, and examined by
Mr. Harrison.

Q. How long have you known Trinidad? A. I have been acquainted with it since 1803.

3

Q. How long have you known the Spanish West
Indies? A. Since I was born, I was born in them.

Q. Where were you born? A. I was born in
South America.

Q. Are the laws which govern the West India
Islands belonging to Spain, in force there? A. They
are.

Q. In what situation were you? A. I was
in several. I was brought up to the law.

Q. In what character did you practise? A. I
practised as an advocate.

Q. Where did you practise? A. At St. Dafie,
is the new kingdom of Grenada.

Q. Have you been in various parts of the Spanish
West Indies? A. I have.

Q. Will you be so good as to enumerate them?
A. I have been in the greatest part of Grenada, in
Caraccas, in the isle of Portorico, in Trinidad, Ha-
vannah, and Cuba.

Q. Are you acquainted with the laws? A. I
think I am.

Q. Have you studied them as a profession?
A. Yes I have.

Q. Take this book and state to the court and jury
if that is a book which you considered as containing
the laws for the government of the Indies? A. Yes.

Lord Ellenborough. " What is the name?

Witness. The Recopilacion of the laws of India relating to South America. Ordered to be printed by
his Catholic Majesty King Charles II.

Q. Do you know the contents ?   A. Yes, I do.

Q. Is there any thing in that book, which jus-tifies the infliction of torture?   A. Not to my knowledge.

Q. From all your acquaintance with that book, under its authority, can torture be practised ? A. I never heard of any thing of the kind or practised to my knowledge.   I never saw any such thing.

Q. Is it in Grenada or Caraccas where the appeal lies ?

A. No, at Caraccas ; I was only established for a few years.

Q. In Cuba is it practised ?   A. I was only two months at Cuba, but I saw nothing of it there.

Q. Did you ever see it practised in any of the places you have mentioned ?   A. In none of them.

Q. Did you ever hear of it in any part of the Spanish West Indies, upon, or by any persons ? A. No, I think not.

Q. In your judgment as a lawyer could it be done under any authority ?

LORD ELLENBOROUGH.   Q. Could it have been the general practice without your having a knowledge of it ?   A. No, certainly not.

LORD ELLENBOROUGH.   Q. Did you see any in-strument for its infliction in the goals?   A. No, my Lord : I never did see any of them.

Q. In your judgment as a lawyer could torture be inflicted by law ?

LORD ELLENBOROUGH. " You may not put that

question: You may ask him if there be any law which authorises its being put in practice."

Q. Do you as a lawyer know of any law which justifies putting to the torture?

MR. GARROW. Q. According to the law as you know it could torture be legally inflicted.

LORD ELLENBOROUGH. Q. Do you know of a law which authorises torture to be inflicted? A. There is an ancient edict dated in 1260 which does authorise it; but it is the law of Partidas, belonging to Old Spain; it is now not endeavoured to be put in practice.

MR DALLAS, " That is not evidence."

LORD ELLENBOROUGH. " He says he does not know of the torment being any where inflicted, and he has made a study of the law as long back as 1260, he says there is a law which does authorise it, but that it has gotten into disrepute: that fact is in evidence."

Q. Do you consider persons bound by it? A. No, I do not.

LORD ELLENBOROUGH. Was it considered a binding law in your time? A. I believe not.

MR. GARROW. Q. Then you find written in a treatise of ancient date something which might justify torture? A. Yes, there is.

LORD ELLENBOROUGH, It is too much to rest the law on an ancient writing in the year 1260. You may find something of the same kind in the old English laws."

MR. DALLAS. " It would be extremely strong if our case rested on the ancient law of 1260."

LORD ELLENBOROUGH. "I am aware of it, and this is a point which must be left to the jury to decide. if there be a law in Spain which authorises the torture. I thought it would be found to be the clear law; but we have conflicting testimony. We cannot find evidence but we must find facts."

MR. DALLAS. "We must then, my Lord, go through the evidence obtained under the mandamus.

The Witness cross-examined by Mr. Dallas.

Q. How long have you practised as advocate?
A. For two years in St. Daffie's Court.

Q. Then your experience is only from that time?
A. I must tell you, that by the laws of Spain, those who are to study the law are obliged to practice for five years in the inferior courts; then they are examined before the full council; after I was approved I practised for two years."

Q. Then two years is the whole length of your experience? A. It is.

Q. Is there any part of that book which directs what legal proceeding shall be had when a person is suspected of robbery? A. I do not know; it is something difficult to say; I have not read them lately, and the work is in three Volumes.

Q. I want to know if these books contain any direction to a criminal judge how to proceed in matters of accusation? A. I am not prepared for that question; but notwithstanding I will tell you with consideration.

o

(The Witness for some time carefully inspected the work.)

Q. Will you swear that there is from beginning to end of these three volumes a single page prohibiting the practice of torture? A. I will not swear there is not in these three volumes: I think not. I cannot tel.

Q. When did you arrive in the country? A. I came in the year 1799, I believe: I am not quite certain. I arrived before the peace was concluded. The peace between France and Spain.

Q. Did you give in your name at the Alien Office?

LORD ELLENBOROUGH. "You must not ask him that, because he may involve himself in penalties."

Q. Did you pass at any time under the name of Smith? A. Yes, I did: it came to the knowledge of Lord Hobart before the peace was concluded.

Q. Have you at any time been employed in taking examinations against General Picton? A. No, sir; I believe not. I was not employed officially.

Q. Upon your oath, have you not been employed by Colonel Fullarton, to take the examinations of different persons? A. Colonel Fullarton wished to have the assistance of my opinion, but I would not give it.

Q. Have you, or have you not been employed by Colonel Fullarton to take the depositions of different persons against General Picton? A. I was employed as interpreter to translate them.

Q. By Mr. GARROW. You translated the evidence of the witnesses who spoke Spanish? A. Yes I did.

LORD ELLENBOROUGH. "We will now proceed to the evidence under the mandamus."

The depositions of Don Aliero Begorat were then put in and read by the clerk of the court.

In answer to the first interrogatory enquiring of Signior Begorat if he were the judge who tried Louisa Calderon; he answered, that the judge who received the first complaint was General Picton, and he committed Louisa Calderon to goal on the 3rd. of December, 1801. He attended to the business twenty-two days.

In answer to the second interrogatory, demanding if the defendant ever talked with Signior Begorat during the proceedings of the measures to be adopted, it was said that he did not, he only asked if the man who committed the robbery were discovered.

The third demanded, if he were a graduated lawyer, which was answered in the negative.

The fourth asked how then he could accept the office of Alcalde. To this Signior Begorat replied that, to hold the situation of Alcalde, it was unnecessary; that it is not required that the judge should write or read, and that if the person elected refused to accept the office, he was liable to a heavy penalty.

The Fifth interrogatory enquired if the goaler were directed to take charge of Louisa Calderon, and if, by Signior Begorat's order, she were put upon the picquet. Replication was made to this: that the deponent had not sufficient authority to give the order, and was obliged to consult the superior tribunal; he therefore ordered the Escribano to apply to the higher court to obtain leave, observing that the suspicions were extremely strong against Louisa Calderon, and telling the General that, putting her on the picquet, would probably make her confess. To this the governor answered that she should be put to the torture.

The Seventh demanded if he consulted General Picton in the affair; to which the reply was, that the rule of law obliged him to do so.

It was asked by the eighth interrogatory if it were necessary to consult a graduated advocate. To this it was answered that he could not have put Louisa on the picquet with his authority.

The ninth, tenth, eleventh, and twelfth interrogatories contained nothing material. The thirteenth enquired what were the modes of torture. The deponent replied that the methods were not defined, but that they might be known by reference to the Bobadilla. It was inflicted according to the strength of the accused, and that Signior Begorat ordered but a slight torture to Louisa Calderon.

The fourteenth interrogatory stated, that the infliction was to be at the discretion of the judge; and the fifteenth gave a description of the picquet.

The depositions of Francisco de Farfan were then read.

No material answer was given to any of the interrogatories, excepting to the third and the twenty-second, the first of which placed the superior tribunal on General Picton; and the last stated that the crime of Louisa Calderon by law authorised the application of torture.

Mr. Dallas. " That, my lord, is all we read."

Lord Ellenborough. "Do you call parol evidence to the practice of torture?

Mr. Dallas. " We have no other evidence, my lord, on the subject."

Lord Ellenborough. " As I stopped, Mr. Dallas, when the special verdict was agreed to, I now wish to hear him on the contradictory evidence."

Mr. Garrow. " I thought Mr. Dallas had concluded his address."

Mr. Dallas. " I certainly had not, for I understood it to be a discretional verdict."

Lord Ellenborough. " I cannot put down in the special verdict contradictory evidence, that must be left to the Jury, and thus will decide, if the law of torture existed, at the time the defendant committed the offence, and they will dispose of it either one way or the other. If they are of opinion that such a law did exist, then it can be inserted in the special verdict."

Mr. Dallas. " May it please your lordship. Gentlemen of the Jury, I can have no objection to take the course marked out for me, (Interrupted by)

Mr. Garrow. " Before you go on I must state, now we are in this stage, that one of the witnesses for the prosecution, under the mandamus states, that he had known the island 10 years, and never saw any person tortured or any instrument for the purpose. I should wish that to be read."

Lord Ellenborough. " At the time you called Vargas you said that you had finished your case."

Mr. Garrow. " When I stated that, my lord, I mentioned that I had many witnesses to prove that no torture was ever practised. However I have no wish that it should be read."

Lord Ellenborough. " We go to the Jury, then, merely upon this question."

Mr. Dallas. " May it please your lordship. Gentlemen of the Jury. The case is now confined to a single point, and I have no objection to pursue the course chalked out for me, by his lordship, other, therwise I should have been entitled again to address you. Reduced as the case now stands to a single question, I will state to you the only subject for your consideration, which is a mere matter of fact, viz; whether, if upon the evidence you can on your oath declare, that by the laws of Spain, by the laws of that particular colony, and in the peculiar situation of the defendant, torture was not applicable, and whether the criminal judge could not in any instance be justified in ordering its infliction. I own I had upon this point made an extremely strong case, for the evidence did not consist of persons who had practised in any Spanish colonies, but I produced before books, some of them commentaries on the laws of Spain, by distinguished Civilians; others a collection of the different decisions which had taken place, from time to time, and added this most important fact, that these were books which in the course of criminal justice, the judge would have been under the necessity of consulting in the colony, for the due administration of justice. I cannot forget that I called before you Mr. Gloster, who tells you that these are the books which are constantly resorted to, and consulted by the advocates who practise, and which are the standing incontrovertible authorities in the island of Trinidad. With what effect then can it be said that his experience was obtained, only since the year 1803, a time subsequent to the transaction; for it would require more ingenuity than is possessed by my learned friend, (and at the same time, I know that he possesses more than ever belonged to any man but himself) to convince you that all the different columes of authority, have found their way into Trinidad, between the year 1802, when the torture was inflicted, and 1803, when Mr. Gloster arrived in the island. I therefore place my foot upon this ground, on the stability and firmness of which I can confidently rely; that if Mr. Gloster found the books in the different courts of justice, and saw the judges and advocates reforming to them day by day, finding them there in 1803, would be satisfactory, convincing, and conclusive evidence, to any reasonable mind, that these were the authorities, that for a long period before that time, such judges and advocates had been in the habit of consulting.

" If the single question were, if these were books considered and consulted as authorities in Trinidad, it would be next to impossible that you could for a moment entertain any doubt upon it; and then I may be entitled to state that the present case in point of proof, stands before you under these circumstances and in this light. There are a great number of books produced, ancient and modern, some of them being as recent as 1773, and others dated in 1795. We have it in proof before us, that by the general law of Spain, torture may be administered; and then I should be glad to hear what is the observation to be made on the testimony of the gentleman who tells you he recollects an ancient law which passed in the year 1260, and afterwards informs you that that law does not exist in Spain.

" Therefore, what becomes of all the remarks which have been so pressed upon your attention: they must all go for nothing. And I call upon you, in this case, in which Colonel Fullarton is the actual prosecutor; I say, I call upon you, my case standing upon the facts, to say, if I have not made out that, that there is not the smallest foundation for the bold and rash assertion of Vargas, that the infliction of torture depends merely on the ancient law of Spain, in 1260, which has fallen into disrepute and derision;

but on the contrary, I assert, that down to the year 1795, the authorities state that there is a Spanish law, which law justifies the infliction of torture.

" With respect to Spain itself, we have it then thus : what is the different situation in which the Spanish law stands in the colonies. You have had an immense body of evidence to shew that torture might be applied to criminals, and that books were published for the express information of the judge who was to try the cause, assuring him that by the laws of Old Spain torture might be applied.

" But have my friends endeavoured to shew that the laws of the colony are different from those of the mother country ? No, they have made no such vain attempt, and, therefore, when I find it laid down as an universal principle, that in Spain torture may be applied, I then stand upon that general rule, that as by the laws of the mother country it is applicable, it is also applicable in the colonies in particular cases. But it does not alone stand here, for the law is established from the examination of a graduate of *two years* standing.

" I admit nothing is to be found with respect to torture, in the books for the government of the colonies, and on the footing of one book called the Recopilacion ; it is for you to declare that you are satisfied on the testimony of this one witness, against all the other evidence in the depositions, and that there is no such thing as torture admitted with respect to accomplices in a crime.

P

" But, gentlemen, you cannot forget the question I asked the witness, Vargas, this *juris consult*. I called on him to tell me if in that book stated to be for the government of the colonies, any thing were to be found respecting the application of torture to accomplices. The witness turned over page by page, and concluded his testimony without being able to refer either me or you to any passage respecting the infliction of torture. I, therefore, gentlemen, call upon you to find out in the whole book any single page which prohibits the infliction of torture.

" My evidence is possitive on the subject, and asserts torture to be the general practice; whereas, they have only referred you to the book to which I have just alluded. Gentlemen, I scorn to make any observations upon the last witness for the prosecution, he has gone under the name of Smith, and now comes before you under another. You must likewise be acquainted with the enmity existing between Colonel Fullarton and General Picton.

" I, therefore, gentlemen, leave the case in your hands; it is for you to judge of the evidence adduced on the one side and the other; but I do most firmly believe, that, weighing the testimony of the different witnesses, you cannot declare upon the oaths which you have taken, that no law did exist, which authorizes the application of torture."

Mr. GARROW then rose, and addressed the jury as follows: " Gentlemen of the jury. It is with extreme concern I find myself again called upon to address you on this most important case; but the mode in which the defence has been conducted, makes it the more indispensible for me to trouble you with some observations. My friend has been, as he always is to me, extremely courteous, and he is one of the last men disposed to volunteer in making harsh observations upon the witnesses called in opposition to the case he has to support : nothing but the greatest distress would have induced him to make the severe remarks upon the learned gentleman termed by him a *juris consult.*

" Let us now proceed, gentlemen, to observe to what credit Mr. Vargas is entitled. He gives us this account of himself. He was born in the Spanish dominions of South America, was educated to the study of the law, and has been in practice for two years. Two years, says my friend, is the whole of his experience. Now I think it is a little unfortunate that he should at this time be contrasted with Mr. Gloster, the Attorney General in Trinidad.

" The one man was bred up to letters and the science of the laws of his country, skilled in the language in which those laws are written, and like all other men in his country who follow his profession, has been under the necessity of practising, first in courts of inferior jurisdiction, and then of being examined in a full court; and having obtained a certificate of his fitness, he is permitted to act in the concerns of others. He does not assert, there was no law which inflicted torture, but that on the contrary, there was

such a law of Old Spain; but he says the colonies were
not governed by the laws of Spain, but in by a book
which was printed in the year 1783, expressly published for the government of the colonies, and particularly for the increase of the population and commerce of the port of Spain; and he says, looking at
this and other codes, he finds no justification of the application of torture. Upon being asked again, he says,
there is an edict in 1260, by which the torture is justified, and he stated to you, that during the whole
course of his practice, he had never known, heard of,
or seen the infliction of the torture; and he went on
to state, that as he believed it was formerly the law,
the good sense of the times, and the ridicule applied
to that method of extracting the truth by torture had
abolished it from society."

" Gentlemen, he did not state that there was no
such law, but that he had never known any infliction
of torture in the West India Dominions of Spain.
This is the man, whom my friend has treated in this
so derogatory a manner.

" Who has been called on the other side skilled in
the law of Spain? You have had Mr. Gloster, gentlemen, who says he can scarcely read Spanish, and
disclaims all knowledge of the law; and when a
passage was given him to translate, he said there were
many legal phrases which he could not understand, and that he was unable to read the Spanish language without a dictionary. This gentleman is the
Juris Consult, on whose authority you are to find

that there is a law by which torture may be inflicted. The passages from the books were read, and were rightly read, because his Lordship has received them, but my Lord will give me leave to say, that they but just come within the limits prescribed, for testimony.

" Gentlemen, you have Mr. Gloster brought before you when a verdict of guilty is to be recorded against the defendant, to tell you, that he has seen the books in question on the table of a person resembling in office our notary public, and that for that reason, and for that alone, he believes them to be books of authority, excepting, that he observed them before the council of which he had the honour to be a member, and saw them referred to, but he never examined them himself, and he was totally ignorant if the laws were administered according to those authorities.

" Gentlemen, is this the way in an English court a defendant is to be justified? When I demand your verdict of guilty, I am sure you will say I ask for nothing more than I ought to receive for the satisfaction of your consciences; and there is nothing more for you to say, than guilty, or not guilty, justified, or criminal. Supposing you should be of opinion, that General Picton has been misinformed, his own duty should have pointed out the path he was to have pursued."

LORD ELLENBOROUGH. " That I shall leave for the motion for a new trial."

. MR. GARROW. " Yes, my lord. Gentlemen,

I did not mean to bring the defendant before you with a halter round his neck, desiring you to pull it tight; no, gentlemen, his counsel does the most he can for him, to say he was misinformed. If he has been misinformed, he is not the less guilty. He erred from the faithful discharge of his duty. He was placed in the island in the highest official situation; and it would have been considered a libel upon his character to have supposed, that he would have acted so, even if he were authorised, the crime being so contrary to the dictates of humanity.

"The old regulations were to remain in force until his majesty's pleasure should be known, and until new laws were issued.

"It was thought that it might be extremely inconvenient to govern his majesty's recently acquired subjects by new laws, and therefore the defendant was directed to rule them by those which at the time of the cession of the island were in force.

"My friend tells you, that General Picton is neither a lawyer or a civilian. No, gentlemen, he is not; but he is a British governor, and had an English heart beating in his bosom; and when he saw the unhappy victim of cruelty in that dreadful situation, he ought to have required no legal advice, no auditor, and no assessor, to have told him of its illegality."

MR. DALLAS. "I understand, my lord, the single question to be, if by the Spanish law, torture can be applied; and therefore my learned friend is not entitled to make a general address."

LORD ELLENBOROUGH. " The question of torture is the first, and if that is found against you Mr. Dallas, then there must be a verdict of guilty; but if there be a law which authorises it, then it will come to the point, of how far the defendant has acted according to the law: but if there be no such law, then the latter question will not be agitated. The proper point now is, as to the existence of the law; and by that, the other topics will be done away, but otherwise, all will arise. There is a consent for a special verdict, if there had not been contrary evidence on the subject; and it leads either to a mere verdict of guilty, or to the special verdict. I only desired that the question of malice should be done away, because every thing that is done contrary to law is construed to be *malo animo*, and malice is implied. I therefore think the counsel for the prosecution is entitled to a general address."

MR. GARROW. " Gentlemen of the Jury, I am extremely surprised at this interruption, and the more so, because there never was a man, and never will be, who more readily submitted to the decision of a point by any learned judge. I was persuaded, gentlemen, that I was entitled to a general address, but I shall refrain, because I feel that it is unnecessary. I am not now addressing you on the footing of a special, but upon that of a general verdict.

But, gentlemen, I told you I meant to contend that this was to be a verdict of guilty, or not guilty, justified or unprotected. I believe those are the words I used.

" I assert that the defendant cannot possibly be justified; for unless you find a special law, which would have authorised the former governor, in that case General Picton must be found generally guilty of inflicting most barbarously the torture charged in this indictment. According to the doctrine endeavoured to be established by the defendant, a judge, in the case of witnesses not telling the truth, or prevaricating, may order torment to be inflicted, until evidence be discovered to support the case.

" But, gentlemen, with respect to the picture, which has been stated to have inflamed your minds, I directly assert, that I never exhibited it until the counsel for the defendant gave his permission. I ask nothing of your passions; I require nothing at your hands, unless the strong facts force you to give your verdict against a British governor."

It has been said that the judge may, in his discretion, inflict torture; but, at the time, no person is to be present but the Judge, the Escribano, and the executioner, and it is to be inflicted in a place apart from all witnesses, and where nobody is to hear what passes. I complain, gentlemen, that the defendant was not present. If those were always by who give the order for the torture, I believe there would be fewer victims sacrificed, and I will do the defendant the justice to think that if he had been present at this horrid transaction, instead of Begorat, if he had seen the unhappy creature in the first moments of her agony, when, with lips quivering with pain, she was making the extorted confession, the watch would not have gone its appointed round, but he would have been glad to restore her to happiness and her friends. I complain that he first consigned her to a dungeon, and then gave the bloody order to be executed by another.

" But, to confine myself to the important question in the case, if there was such a law existing as authorised the infliction of torture. By the laws relating to the Spanish West Indies, nothing is said concerning torture; but then, says my friend, there is a positive contradiction of it.

" Gentlemen, it remains to the disgrace of the British character, that the only person who ever gave such an order, was the defendant; and the evidence brings it home to him; and, notwithstanding they had full notice of this prosecution for a considerable number of years, they have not produced to you one Spanish Governor to prove that torture was ever known in the Indies. Here persons were standing by to record what was extorted from Louisa Calderon, and even when Mr. Gloster was asked if he ever knew torture to have been administered to any body, under any circumstances, ' No,' he says, ' he never heard of such a thing.' The Frenchman who was called, disclaimed all knowledge of such horrid transactions, and cried out with abhorrence, 'Never, never, heard of such a thing.' When General Picton was beating up for evidence in the year 1803, he examined every gaol, and place of confinement, to discover any old musty book, which might contain something concerning the use of torture, and these are the produce of his labours, these are the authorities which has to day been produced ; and, if you disbelieve this evidence, you must slight that best of all commentators, experience, which, upon the present occasion, tells you that no such law did exist.

" We produce the very man who was present at the time the torture was inflicted, and he tells you he had lived in the island for ten years, and, during that time, was well acquainted with the gaol, and he never used or heard of such a thing as an instrument of torture till the arrival of the defendant. We cannot but all lament that military punishment should be necessary to be inflicted upon the hardy soldier ; yet, as I stated to you before, the humanity of the British character, when the picquet is employed, has given the unhappy sufferer a resting place for his arm, by which means he is enabled to support himself while standing upon the instrument. This was not allowed to Louisa Calderon, and, when you find that General Picton is the sole inventor of this kind of torture, will you have the least doubt in saying that he is not justified by the written law. This case reminds me of the barbarous custom of throwing witches into a large cistern of water. If they were drowned, they were considered guiltless, but, if they were able to support themselves in the water, they were held to be witches, and were accordingly burnt. Whipping was often inflicted in Trinidad, and tying whipcord round a criminal's thumbs; but this is done as a punishment, and not with a view of extorting a confession from him. This is supported by the testimony of the witnesses. The punishment or torture, which would be nothing to a drayman, would be death to the delicate female who has this day been produced before you; and it is a fact, admitted on all sides, that torture was never known in the island until the arrival of the defendant.

" Gentlemen, you will take into your minds the great consolation the defendant will have in reflecting that he is the first person in the island who erected any instrument of torture for human nature. Even if the defendant had told you that his Escribano had said it was the law, and desired him to inflict it, then I should say there was something like a justification for his conduct: but this is not done, and if he had known nothing else, he must have been aware of the extremely tender age of Louisa Calderon, and ought not to have consigned her to such barbarous cruelty.

" In the happy laws by which Great Britain is ruled, it is not permitted that any person should be convicted upon his own extorted confession, and if it be attempted to be produced against a prisoner, the

3

judge alway interferes, and asks the party if it was obtained from him either by threats or promises, or if any thing was said which could place him in a better or a worse situation ; and if it appears that there was, the judge would say that he could not receive the confession.

" My friend reminds of a part of the evidence, not less material than the rest ; I mean that of Farfan, who was procured by Mr. Gloster, and he states that he never heard of a law which inflicted torture upon any person. If, therefore, gentlemen, you find, as I confidently trust you will, that there is no such law as warrants the torture ; in that case you will say the defendant is guilty of having wilfully, maliciously, and with a view to oppress Louisa Calderon, committed this offence against the laws of the island in which he was placed as governor."

LORD ELLENBOROUGH. " What is Farfan ?"

MR. GARROW. " I believe, my lord, he holds some office under the government."

LORD ELLENBOROUGH. " Gentlemen of the jury, I would advise by all means to divest yourselves of every thing which can inflame your minds, so that you may give impartial attention to the question in the present case, which is, What was the law which governed the island of Trinidad at the time of the cession to His Majesty's forces under Sir Ralph Abercrombie ? The point before you unites in itself the law of the land, and it is for you to consider, if the power of inflicting personal torture was included in the authority of the governor. The first matter of the case in proof with regard to the law, was, His Majesty's instructions to the defendant, and the question, is what was then the subsisting law which regulated the island. By them it appears that the articles of capitulation were to remain in force, but I think, that contains nothing to elucidate the point. It proceeds to state, that all the contracts made before the capture of Trinidad, were to remain binding, that individuals might not lose their profits upon the sale of commodities, and this stipulation seems to have been performed agreeably to the terms of the surrender. The fifth article in the instructions to General Picton states, that the ancient laws which governed the island at the capture, were to remain in force subject to any directions which should be received from this country.

"The seventeenth article states that it is His Majesty's will and pleasure for the present, that the same courts of judicature which subsisted previously to the surrender, should be continued in the exercise of their different jurisdictions in all criminal and civil causes, and should proceed according to the laws of the said island ; and such as were exercised by the Spanish governor in like manner were to be executed as before the surrender of Trinidad. That, gentlemen, was to be the limit of his authority, and the measure by which he was to administer justice to the inhabitants.

"This brings us to a very nice point, viz. in fact, what was the criminal law of the country? The island of Trinidad is not any part of Old Spain, but was annexed to it at some time or other. But we have no evidence upon what terms it was annexed, by what laws it was associated, or what were the regulations which subsisted on the island, at the time it was so annexed.

"The Royal Schedula is a publication which contains some circumstances respecting the regulations on the subject; of criminal justice, and another book, called the Recopilacion, has been likewise produced, which gives a code of laws for the government of the Spanish West Indies. But that publication does not make any mention of torture, and therefore the right of applying it can only subsist on the authorities, if it subsist at all, some of which authorities certainly state by reference to law books, that the infliction of torture is a part of the power of judges.

"We are not made acquainted during the proceedings of the cause, at what time the island of Trinidad was associated to the Spanish West India dominions, whether at the time of the discoveries made by Columbus, or otherwise, and what laws were then assigned for its government.

"But it appears, by a witness who has known the island for thirty-two years, who was born in the Indies belonging to the Crown of Spain, and who was likewise an Alcalde; by Mr. Nugent, who

speaks to his acquaintance with the island since
the year 1786, and by all the evidence, that to
their knowledge they never heard of a single instance in which torture had been applied in Trinidad; and, therefore, in the absence of living witnesses
to speak to the applications of the torture; the
question is without knowing on what terms the
island was conjoined to the mother country, what
were the laws of the island, and if torture made a
part of them ?

" Mr. Gloster has stated the law to you on many
subjects, from books which are treated as authorities, but the existence of them, and reference to
them, can certainly not extend beyond the period
of time that he himself was acquainted with them.
He however went to Trinidad in 1803, and the punishment was inflicted in 1801, by Begorat, who
himself tells you, that he recollects the first instance of torture was in the barrack yard, upon
the soldiers. This experience therefore, weighs a-
gainst the law as in the books, for not only it does
not appear to have been used, but the instrument
seems first to have been introduced in 1801, under
the directions of the defendant himself.

" But the law of Spain may have been in all its
parts in practice at Trinidad, and these books applying to the regulations of Old Spain, furnish no
light upon the subject; they only give us the laws
of the mother country, and not the rules for the
government of the islands. The Curea Philippica

likewise contains passages relative to inflicting the question. It says, ' in the same manner that it is applicable to the delinquent, it is likewise applicable to the witness who varies or prevaricates in his evidence.' Without going through each particular situation in which torture is to be inflicted, I think you can take that only to be the existing law of Spain, and we may assume, that by the general law of that country it may be lawful to quit it in practice.

" The means of compelling a party to plead guilty or not guilty was abolished in the year 1804, when the recorder was attending the Old Bailey sessions. That law obliged a party accused to plead to an indictment, under a penalty, which, indeed, was much like putting a person to the torture : but here the question is, if the torture were included in the law of Trinidad, and if such law have not been acted upon, it still does not obviate the point whether such was the existing law of the island at the time of the capitulation.

" Mr. Gloster gives you the authorities, and tells you, that they are all books which are considered to relate to the laws of Spain; and so they might be, without effecting the present question. The law of Jamaica, and various other dependences on the British government, is totally different from that of the mother country ; and, therefore, to produce law-books, which regulate this kingdom, would not draw the conclusion that Jamaica, also, was governed by them. The question comes before us in the total absence of all evidence. Neither Farfan or Gourville recollect torture being applied, but the latter remembers the circumstance of tying the thumbs of criminals. Mr. Nugent, who knew the island since 1786, and who completed twenty years stay in the island, if we calculate to the present time, never heard of the practice: but it is for you, gentlemen, to take his evidence to what extent you may think of it.

" Mr. Vargas states himself to have been an advocate for two years, and has visited a number of places. He says he has been at Caraccas, Portorico, Cuba, and other Spanish dominions and likewise in Trinidad; and he swears that he has never known or heard of an instance of the infliction of torture: but he mentions an edict of 1260, but he says it has even fallen into disrepute in Spain: and I think you are to assume that it is the law of Spain, and therefore can have no relation to the present enquiry, whether it was the subsisting law of the island.

" Therefore, gentlemen, such being the law of Old Spain, the question is, if in the absence of all usage for thirty-two years, you are enabled to say that the application of torture was the existing law of the island of Trinidad at the time of the capitulation. If you are of opinion that it was the subsisting law, it will be inserted in the special verdict; if you think otherwise, and that no such law was in

R

force, I shall be glad to communicate my sentiments to you farther upon the subject."

After about five minutes consideration, the Jury said, that they were of opinion no such law was in force.

LORD ELLENBOROUGH. "Then, gentlemen, of course General Picton cannot derive any protection from the circumstance of a supposed law, and finding that there is no such law, your verdict must be that he is guilty."

A verdict of GUILTY was then recorded.

Mr. Dallas now intimated his intention of moving for a new trial, on the ground that there was no proof of malice; or supposing the defendant to have acted contrary to law, the mistake arose from improper advice, for which he was not answerable, being an act done in the execution of his office.

LORD ELLENBOROUGH. "You will have the benefit of taking all objections on your motion for a new trial."

FINIS.

Printed by Bewick and Clarke,
Aldersgate-street.

CPSIA information can be obtained
at www.ICGtesting.com
Printed in the USA
BVHW011556190721
612308BV00014B/655